JERUSALEM

JERUSALEM

Caught in Time

Colin Osman

NEW YORK UNIVERSITY PRESS
Washington Square, New York

First published in the U.S.A. in 2000 by
NEW YORK UNIVERSITY PRESS
Washington Square
New York, NY 10003

Library of Congress Cataloging-in-Publication Data

Jerusalem : caught in time / [compiled by] Colin Osman.
    p.   cm.
Includes bibliographical references and index.
ISBN 0–8147–6200–X (cloth : alk. paper)
1. Jerusalem—History—19th century—Pictorial works. 2.
Photography—Palestine—History—20th century. I. Osman, Colin.

DS109.925 .J46 2000
956.94'4203—dc21

99–053019

Editor: **Emma Hawker**
Production: **Nick Holroyd**
Design: **David Rose**

Map of Jerusalem on page vi drawn by Geoprojects (UK) Ltd., © 1999

Printed in Lebanon

Previous page
James McDonald. The Dome of the Chain. 1864–5.
The Dome of the Chain is a small dome that lies directly east of one door
of the Dome of the Rock. Legend states that a chain once hung there
which could not be grasped by anyone giving false testimony.

Contents

MAP OF JERUSALEM

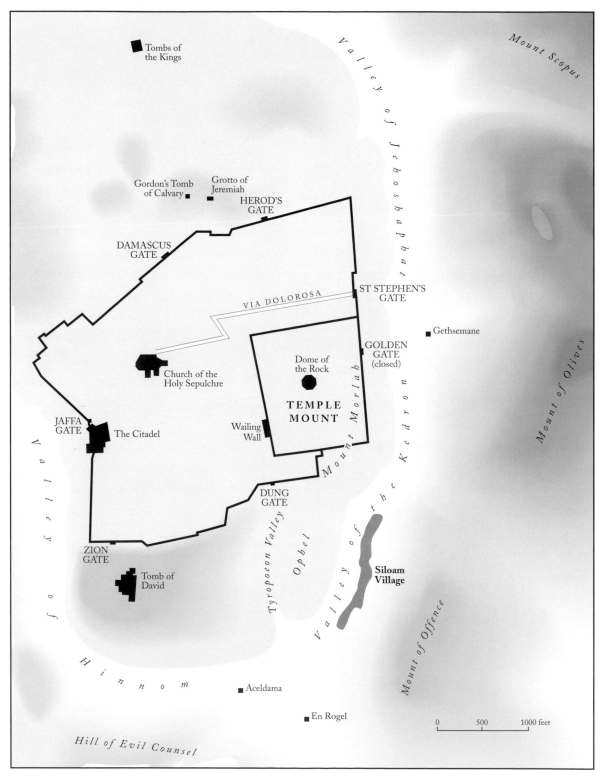

Tombs of
the Kings

Gordon's Tomb
of Calvary

Grotto of
Jeremiah

HEROD'S
GATE

DAMASCUS
GATE

Valley of Jehoshaphat

Mount Scopus

VIA DOLOROSA

ST STEPHEN'S
GATE

Gethsemane

Dome of
the Rock

GOLDEN
GATE
(closed)

Church of the
Holy Sepulchre

Mount Moriah

Mount of Olives

TEMPLE
MOUNT

JAFFA
GATE

The Citadel

Wailing
Wall

Valley of the Kedron

DUNG
GATE

Tyropoeon Valley

Ophel

ZION
GATE

**Siloam
Village**

Tomb of
David

Valley of

Mount of Offence

H i n n o m

Aceldama

En Rogel

0   500   1000 feet

Hill of Evil Counsel

Preface

Even though the Palestine Exploration Fund (PEF), from whose superb collections most of the photographs in this book are drawn, is firstly an archaeological society, archaeology is not the subject of this book. Nor does the book concern itself with politics or religion; rather, it is purely and simply about photography.

The PEF has provided us with a large and very fine collection which includes a great treasury of Ordnance Survey photographs. From 1864 to after 1880, Jerusalem, Palestine, Sinai and Transjordan were surveyed and mapped by the officers and men of the Royal Engineers, who received funding from the PEF. Along with the surveyors were two men, Sergeants McDonald and Phillips, who were seconded to photography. Between them they produced the first photographic survey of the Holy Land and a unique record of the country. In later years the survey was to be continued by such notables as Lieutenant Kitchener (who, it has to be said, was a better soldier than photographer) and a certain T. E. Lawrence, also better known for other activities.

The PEF was a part of the Victorian religious zeal that characterized British Protestant activity in the Holy Land at the end of the last century. Founded in 1865 with the aim of promoting research into the archaeology, manners and customs, topography, geology and natural sciences of biblical Palestine, the PEF now has a history rich in association with the outstanding names of biblical exploration: Wilson, Warren, Conder, Kitchener of Khartoum, Schumacher, Petrie, Bliss, Macalister, Woolley, T. E. Lawrence, Garstang, Crowfoot and Kenyon. The projects on which they worked, such as Jerusalem (1868–9), the Survey of Western Palestine (1871–7), and many others, were commissioned by the PEF and have become famous landmarks in the history of biblical archaeology and the exploration of the Holy Land. The comments of Dame Kathleen Kenyon in her book of personal excavations in the 1950s, *Digging Up Jerusalem*, sums it up well:

'The middle years of the nineteenth century constituted a period in which the great civilizations of Western Asia were being revealed by the spade of the archaeologist and the interest aroused was very great … It was in this climate of excitement at the revelation of remains contemporary with the Biblical record of the history of the kingdoms of Judah and Israel that the Palestine Exploration Fund came into existence … The objects of the Fund were the "accurate and systematic investigation of the archaeology, the topography, the geology and physical geography, the manners and customs of the Holy Land for Biblical Illustration."'

Note the importance of the last words 'for

Biblical Illustration', these should be taken literally. The first committee included an archbishop, four bishops, four deans, two dukes, three earls, three other peers and the Speaker of the House of Commons, not to mention the fact that Queen Victoria was the patron! No wonder they obtained the services not only of the best archaeologists but also the best photographers.

The leading British political figure for 21 of the years that will be covered in this book was Consul James Finn. His task was primarily to look after British subjects but it was government policy to extend Protected Status to Jews who did not have consular representatives in Palestine. That he did this difficult job well is evidenced by the fact that when he was removed from his position, every single rabbi in Jerusalem petitioned Queen Victoria to have him sent back. His wife was very interested in charitable works and outlived her husband by some forty years. She had a keen interest in photography, and though she seems to have taken little active part in it herself, she did own a camera which she loaned to a number of photographers, most notably Mendel Diness, who went on to make a significant contribution to Palestine photography. Mrs Finn also collected

photographs and left her collection to the PEF. She was collecting at a time when no one else was and her contribution to the PEF archives is therefore quite unique.

While archaeological photographs were being sent back to PEF headquarters in London, so other sources of topographical photographs were being added to the archive. Some came from commercial studios but others from enthusiastic amateurs. One such example is James Graham, a brilliant pioneer photographer who was also the local secretary of the London Society for the Promotion of Christianity amongst the Jews.

Some of the most prolific commercial photographers of later decades were the Zangaki brothers of Port Said, and the PEF received the only known negatives of theirs as part of a donation from an unidentified German in Sussex. He gave his photo collection to a local museum that did not know what to do with them, but they were eventually passed to the PEF who realized their importance.

Another contribution came from John Shaw Smith who, although born in England, lived his life in Ireland. He made a long trip through Egypt, Sinai, Petra and the Holy Land with his wife, who recorded their travels in a diary. He made early calotypes of his photographs but very few prints were made and, many years after his death, the original prints and negatives were sold to an American university. However, his daughter had modern prints made from the negatives and presented these to the PEF.

Another important source of photographs for this book was the magazine of the London Society for the Promotion of Christianity amongst the Jews (which utilized the confusing acronym of LJS – the London Jews Society), *The Jerusalem Intelligencia* (called *The Jerusalem Missionary Intelligencia,* or *JMI,* in its heyday). Conversion was one of the Society's aims, but it also founded hospitals and schools which were open to all religions.

The missionaries shared with other evangelists the desire to use images to authenticate the Bible stories. Initially, the magazine, founded in 1835, was illustrated with engravings. It then used engravings made from photographs and then finally, from 1889, half-tone photographs. The monthly issues published in 1904 contained 73 photographs of Palestine. Photographs came from many sources but the *JMI* had three regular 'staff' photographers – Reverend G. Robinson Lees, Reverend Canon J. E. Hanauer and the

layman Charles A. Hornstein. (The latter was Jerusalem-born and perhaps the best photographer of the three.)

My choice from this large and disparate archive has been governed by two ideas. The first was the necessity for good images. Even good photographers have their off-days and fame is therefore no guarantee of inclusion in this book. Secondly, and related to the first notion, was the idea of seeking out less familiar photographers and their less familiar images. Too many histories of photography have concentrated on a handful of individuals, whilst ignoring all others.

In taking advantage of the broad spectrum of the PEF collection, I hope to give a truer picture of photography in Jerusalem than is generally perceived.

COLIN OSMAN
London, 1999

James McDonald.
General view of the city from the north.
James McDonald was a Colour Sergeant with the
Royal Engineers who from 1864–5 photographed
land being surveyed by his companions. This
panorama taken from the north shows the
bleakness outside the city walls.

James Robertson and Felice Beato. St Stephen's Gate. 1857.
The eastern gate leading to the Mount of Olives, and the real start of the Via Dolorosa. Known to non-Christians as the
Lion's Gate because it is said that Suleiman the Magnificent decided to re-build the city walls after a bad dream about lions.

Introduction

The invention of photography in 1839 occurred almost simultaneously in France and Britain. In France, the daguerreotype was a silvered metal image which was unique and could only be reproduced indirectly as an engraving. The earliest photographers in the Near East were the French daguerrotypists Jacques Ittier, Pierre Joly de Lotbinière, Horace Vernet and Hector Horeau, but because their images had to be reproduced as engravings, their work falls outside the scope of this book. The British process was the Talbotype or calotype, invented by William Fox Talbot, an English gentleman scholar. His process produced negatives from which multiple pictures could be made and it is therefore the parent of all modern systems. His negative was ordinary good-quality writing paper sensitized and sometimes made transparent by waxing. Calotype paper cannot be compared with modern emulsions. Each sheet was individually coated by the photographer to his own formula, exposed in a camera with no aperture marks, and then developed by inspection, with the photographer again using his own formula. Yet it was the system used by countless amateurs and produced wonderful atmospheric prints. It was to reign supreme until overtaken by the Scott Archer wet collodion process, first seen in Israel on Francis Frith's first trip in 1856.

The wet collodion negatives were coated on glass and could obviously produce images in much greater detail than the paper negatives. When Francis Frith made his mammoth 16 x 20 inch negatives he produced images that are among the glories of photography. The drawback was that the wet collodion negative actually was wet. A glass plate was coated with wet collodion in a darkroom tent set up beside the camera. It was transferred while still wet to the camera and exposed and then, before it dried, transferred back to the darkroom tent to be developed on the spot. The disadvantages were obvious and many amateurs were slow to abandon the waxed calotypes which could be prepared days or weeks in advance. Even more important was the simple fact that not only was the prepared calotype paper a mere fraction of the weight of the wet collodion glass plate, but it was also unbreakable.

The wet process was to give way in its turn to the dry collodion process, the forerunner of all present-day processes. It came into general use about 1875 and swept the field commercially. Plates could be prepared in advance and developed at leisure. There were some disadvantages: the definition was slightly below the wet process but still far in advance of the calotype. It was also slower than the wet process.

To get some idea of the time involved in taking photographs at the end of the nineteenth century, it is first necessary to consider the speed of photography today. A modern film today is 100 ASA for definition and 400 ASA for indoor use. In Israel today a 100 ASA film might require $\frac{1}{250}$ of a second exposure at an aperture of f11. Given all the processes involved, nineteenth-century calotype exposures could take anything from one second to an incredible two minutes. Even this was faster than the daguerreotype which could take as long as twenty minutes, thus requiring the well-known head clamp for portraits. Compared to the calotype, the wet collodion process allowed much faster exposures – often four to five seconds and on occasion even as little as $\frac{1}{25}$ of a second – so instantaneous photographs were possible, even though the problems of manipulating the wet plates were huge. The comparison of film sensitivity was made even more complicated by the fact that after development wet collodion plates usually needed a further chemical treatment to intensify the image. However, the quality of the best of them was superb and even recently the wet process was used in the printing industry because of the high definition obtainable. The later dry collodion process was far easier to operate but was about six times slower than the wet equivalent, so instantaneous photography again became more difficult. The views were not changed by the slower exposure – except that the leaves of the trees became blurry when the wind blew, and the patient donkeys lost their swishing tails. Portraits remained the same – stilted and stationary.

The positive material for making the prints, albumen-coated paper, had been machine-coated in factories even in the 1860s when negatives were still being hand-coated by the photographer. The improvement in negative material was paralleled by improvements in lens design. The 1886 Rapid Rectilinear lens was a great step forward for exposure times and absence of distortion. The old cameras had no shutters; instead, the lens cap was removed while the photographer counted the seconds. Shutters were now needed for exposures measured in fractions of a second. The biggest change came in 1871 with the development of gelatino-bromide emulsions. These were factory-produced, had a shelf-life of months, even years, and were more sensitive to light. Even if they were still slow by today's standards, they were at least comparable to the materials of today. They were no longer developed by inspection but in darkness, by time and temperature, and the chemicals were often pre-packed in factories. The gelatino-bromide emulsions were exported from factories in Britain, France and Germany and perhaps this partly explains the rise of photographers in Port Said during the 1870s. The commercial market was to be dominated by two of these: Hippolyte Arnoux, who had a floating darkroom on the Suez Canal; and the Zangaki Brothers, whose horse-drawn mobile darkroom can be seen in many of their pictures. Arnoux seems not to have gone north of Port Said but the Zangakis certainly did on what seems to have been an extended tour.

Alexandria as a city on the direct steam boat route to the Holy Land provided a base for many photographers of the area. It was certainly the base from which Luigi Fiorillo made a single tour and it was also a calling place for other visiting

American Colony Photographer. Grotto of Jeremiah and Gordon's Calvary. c. 1900.
This photograph shows Gordon's Calvary and the adjacent Grotto of Jeremiah. It is the skull-like
resemblance to the 'Place of the Skull' (Luke 23: 33) that first led Gordon to his hypothesis.

photographers including Francis Frith and Francis Bedford. The favoured port for those visiting the Holy Land was Beirut, home of the great Bonfils company and of Tancrède Dumas, who became the official photographer to the American Palestine Exploration Society.

The availability and marketing of photographs in Jerusalem was in rather sharp contrast to other areas. Constantinople was a centre for photography and, over the years, thirty photographic studios appeared, many of them in La Grande Rue de Pera. Their largest trade was probably Turkish costume portraits, a tourist favourite. Few photographers ventured beyond their home town. In contrast to Egypt, which had a thriving tourist trade with every Nile boat or hotel lobby thronging with print sellers and shops for the more leisurely buyers, Jerusalem had few hotels and print shops; the latter were also souvenir shops. Frederick Vester is listed in Black's Guide of 1912 as a photographic print seller, and also as a seller of curios, souvenirs, olive wood carvings, *objets de piété* and so on. Near his shop on the Jaffa Road there were at least three or four rivals. That there were photographs of Jerusalem available is evidenced by the fact that when Queen Victoria's fourteen-year-old son Prince Alfred visited the city earlier in 1858, he was asked by Mrs Finn, the British Consul's wife, to make his selection of the sites he would actually like to visit from the photographs in the house.

Murray, Black and Baedeker did recommend photographers in their guide books, but in the 1880s and 1890s chance must have played a large part in deciding which photographer's work was purchased. In 1876 Baedeker put forward Shapira and Bergheim as the best shops. Shapira was not a photographer and Bergheim was a banker of sorts who had also taken photographs for a few years, though he probably sold other photographers' work. He also sold wine and English beer. Black's *Guide* of 1912 lists Frederick Vester, Garabed Krikorian and Chalil Raad. That there were other outlets can be seen from the photographs themselves; for instance, one clearly shows a Jerusalem depot for Bonfils of Beirut. Additional confusion was caused by the fact that identical viewpoints were available from different photographers. In 1856 James Graham taught Mendel Diness to photograph and there are several views where they obviously set up their tripods side by side. In another instance, two almost identical photo-

graphs of 'Arab women in the Middle East' appear signed either by Béchard or Sebah.

Many factors contributed to the final demise of photographic print sales at the end of the century: the decline of the big family album, the rise of the postcard, the advent of the snapshot and the snapshot album. Yet perhaps more than anything else it was the change of attitude as books and magazines could now reproduce photographic images with ease that caused the end of print sales. The photograph was no longer an art object but a consumer expendable. The history of how that change came about has formed the basis of this book.

James McDonald.
General view of the city from the road to Bethany. 1864–5.
Little is known of Sergeant McDonald's training as a photographer but his knowledge of surveying presumably helped make him an expert photographer of panoramic views, made up from up to five or six negatives all exactly matched. The result, as one would expect from an engineer, gives a perfect sense of location.

The Population of Jerusalem

Any attempt to number the population of Jerusalem was doomed from the start. Apart from the expected political pressures, there were religious and administrative problems. The Jews refused to cooperate with any census, fearing a repeat of the pestilence that had fallen on King David after he had 'numbered' Israel and Judea (2 Samuel 24). The Arabs had the more worldly fear that the Turkish rulers would use any census data for taxation purposes and, worse still, for conscription into forced labour. In addition, quota restrictions that had been placed on Jewish immigration had resulted in a large number of illegal residents. The British Consul, James Finn, was one of the many Europeans who made their own estimates of the population of the towns they visited; these estimations are likely to be the most accurate. Yehoushua Ben-Arieh analysed the European estimates for Jerusalem and his findings are recorded in Table 1.

Ben-Arieh ruefully notes that these figures are impossible to reconcile with the official Turkish government figures even though the administrative district, the Qada, in 1871–2 includes the neighbouring 116 villages as well as Jerusalem itself. These villages were mostly populated by Arabs. (See Table 2.)

Year	Muslims	Christians	Jews	Total
1800	4,000	2,750	2,000	8,750
1835	4,500	3,250	3,000	10,750
1840	4,650	3,350	3,000	11,000
1850	5,350	3,650	6,000	15,000
1860	6,000	4,000	8,000	18,000
1870	6,500	4,500	11,000	22,000
1880	8,000	6,000	17,000	31,000
1890	9,000	8,000	25,000	42,000
1900	10,000	10,000	35,000	55,000
1910	12,000	13,000	45,000	70,000

Table 1: Estimates of the Population of Jerusalem
Source: Y. Ben-Arieh, 'The Growth of Jerusalem in the Nineteenth Century' in *Annals of the Association of American Geographers*, 65, 1975, p. 262.

		Muslims	Christians	Jews	Total
Town of Jerusalem	1849	6,148	3,744	1,790	11,682
	1871-72	6,150	4,428	3,780	14,358
Qada of Jerusalem	1881-93	54,364	19,590	7,105	81,059
	1914	70,270	32,461	18,190	120,921

Table 2: The Population of the Town/Qada of Jerusalem 1849–1914 according to Ottoman sources
Source: For Jerusalem see Alexander Schölch, 'The Demographic Development of Palestine, 1850–1882' in *International Journal of Middle East Studies*, 17, 4, 1985. For the Qada (including the town) of Jerusalem see Kamal H. Karpat, *Ottoman Population 1830–1914*, 1985.

What is generally agreed is that from about 1850 the Jews formed the largest religious group in Jerusalem and that by 1870 they outnumbered all other religions combined, though this was only the case in Jerusalem. As far back as 1839, the British Consul had estimated that of the 9,690 Jews in the Holy Land, 5,500 lived in Jerusalem with the rest scattered among nine other towns and villages. Edward Said has pointed out that as late as 1946 the concentration was still on Jerusalem because the total population of Palestine was 1,912,112 of which there were only 608,225 Jews, and that did not change until just before the State of Israel was founded.

The most detailed figures come from 1896:

NON-JEWS	17,360
Muslim Arabs	8,600
Christian Arabs and European Christians	8,760
JEWS	28,112
Ashkenazim	15,074
Sephardim from Asia Minor and Greece	7,900
North African	2,420
Yemenites	1,288
Georgians	670
Bukharians	530
Persians	230
TOTAL POPULATION	45,472

Source: Quoted by Martin Gilbert in *Jerusalem, Illustrated History Atlas*, revised edn, Steimatzky's Agency, Jerusalem, 1978, p. 55.

What is photographically curious is that all the different nationalities of Jews are identified in photographs but, with the exception of the Bedouins, other Arabs are usually represented only as being Muslim. Even the well informed and sympathetic British Consul James Finn called them the 'wild Arabs'. As such the Arabs are invariably pictured waving spears or guns and

Charles A. Horstein. Tent of Salaitah Bedouin c. 1905.

Moses Ephraim Lilien. (Gidal Collection.) 1906.
A group of Yemenite Jews.
If the Holy Land is taken to include Mount Sinai – where Moses received
the law of God – and the Sinai Peninsula, then the Jews of the Yemen are
the only Jews to have lived continuously in the Holy Land.

are usually carefully posed for the photograph. Most of the commercial photographers were more concerned with images that would entertain than with anthropological exactness. It is no surprise then that the same Bedouins appear in photographs from both Egypt and Jerusalem.

The local Bedouins rarely went inside the city walls of Jerusalem, but their encampments and villages surrounded the city and Consul Finn, who knew most of them individually, ensured many a safe passage for travellers and missionaries by using the Bedouins as escorts.

Inter-tribal wars could be serious. In 1854–5, for example, in the struggle for Bedouin supremacy in the Jebel Nabloos, some 3–400 lives were lost and unescorted travellers on the road from Jaffa to Jerusalem had to be well-armed.

Although the Turkish Census included over 100 villages in the Jerusalem district, the most important was Silwan on the hills of Kedron Valley looking across the valley to the Old City, which had a reliable freshwater spring nearby. The villagers came into the city daily with fresh milk and vegetables which could not be grown inside the city. Much was supplied to the shops of the Arab Quarter but there was a lively weekly public market near the Jaffa Gate. Finn states that these sellers possessed a good deal of intelligence and had an immense fund of shrewdness and natural humour. Finn even suggests that these Arabs may have been the lineal descendants of Canaan, the grandson of Noah. They owed no loyalty to the Turkish Sultan, and their only common bond was their commitment to Islam.

Mrs Finn in her *Reminiscences of the 1840s* described the Arabs of the area in the following terms:

'The main population of the country, the so-called "fellahheen" occupied the villages. They were something like the Highland clans, neither leaving their own villages nor intermarrying with other people. Groups of villages within their district were placed in charge of a District Chief. Gradually we made acquaintance with all of these. The wild Arabs on the contrary lived entirely in their own camps. The great tribes were beyond the Jordan eastwards, excepting the Tiyahah on the Philistine Plain. Very rarely did any of them come up to Jerusalem. In the Jordan valley there were some petty tribes, and near the Dead Sea a large one with one thousand fighting men called *taamri*.

As English travellers always wished to visit the Jordan and the Dead Sea, it was necessary to make arrangements for their safety. This had been done by the previous Consul, who settled with the chiefs of Silwan and another village and three of the Jordan tribes that each traveller, on payment of one pound, would be treated as a guest of the tribes. The Bedawy [Bedouin] sense of hospitality is very strong; a host must defend his visitor and his goods, if necessary with his life. Travellers were therefore perfectly safe, even if the escort consisted of one little boy of the tribe. This arrangement brought us into contact with those chiefs.'

James Graham. View from the north-east. 15 September 1855.
James Graham, the lay secretary of the London Society for the
Promotion of Christianity amongst the Jews, was the first
resident photographer in Jerusalem.

James Graham. View from Mount Scopus, north-east of the city. October 1858.
Jerusalem was mostly encircled by valleys which separated the city walls from the surrounding mountains.

L. Fiorillo, No. 153. Gordon's Calvary. c. *1885.*
In 1867 Dr Conrad Schick discovered an ancient tomb near the Grotto of
Jeremiah. General Gordon (of Khartoum etc.), on a visit in 1883, decided
that this must be the true Calvary (or Golgotha) because Christ had to be
buried outside the city walls.

James McDonald. Ancient tombs in the environs of the city. 1864–5.
There were no burials inside the city walls, and this grotto is believed to be a series of
tombs including Gordon's Calvary and the cave in which, according to a tradition
going back to the fourteenth century, the prophet Jeremiah wrote his Lamentations.

W. Hammerschmidt, No. 118. Mount Olivet and the Tombs of the Kedron. c. *1880.*
This is the view down the Valley of the Kedron showing the tombs of Jehoshaphat, Absalom,
St James and Zachariah.

Anon. Rachel's Tomb on the road to Bethlehem. c. 1900.
Rachel was the wife of Jacob (also called Israel) who died in childbirth. The child was called
Benjamin, and Jacob 'set up a pillar upon her grave' (Genesis 35: 16–21). It was the scene of a
regular weekly Jewish pilgrimage.

Anon. Solomon's Pools. c. *1900.*
Solomon's Pools on the road to Hebron may have been the work of Herod the Great. The largest
is 500ft long. They were fed from nearby springs and, via aqueducts, supplied water to Jerusalem
until they were neglected and fell into disrepair.

Anon. View from the Mount of Olives. c. *1905.*
The most famous mountain overlooking Jerusalem is the Mount of Olives, regarded by
Christians as one of their most holy places. The Garden of Gethsemane, where Jesus spent the
night with his apostles prior to his crucifixion, is located here.

Photoglob, Zurich, PZ 15033. Garden of Gethsemane.
The olive trees may date back to the time of Christ but may be self-sown replacements after the
destruction of the trees of Jerusalem by Titus, the companion of St Paul.

James Robertson and Felice Beato. Pillar of Absalom. 1857.
Although there is some doubt as to whether the tomb has anything to do with Absalom, it was
a Jewish tradition to throw a stone at it because of Absalom's rebellion against King David.
The Pillar itself is one of the few buildings that escaped destruction by the Romans in AD 70.

Frank Mason Good, probably No. 1343. Tombs of the Judges. 1875.
The Tombs of the Judges lie just over a mile north of the Damascus Gate. Jewish tradition calls
them the Tombs of the Seventy, connecting them with the seventy elders of the Sanhedrin who
issued Jewish law at the time of the Herodian Temple, though this association is now
considered false because the Old Testament Judges would have been buried in their tribal
territory and there are only a small number of burial places at the site.

James McDonald.
The Tomb of James. 1864–5.
Also known as Bene Hezer, a family of
priests. James was martyred by being
cast down from the nearby temple.

Dr Conrad Schick, 130/2,
No. 1. The Tombs of the Kings. 1869.
The Tombs of the Kings also lie north of the Damascus Gate and
their name is equally misleading because they are actually the tombs of
Queen Helena and her family. This is Helena, Queen of Adiabene
who converted to Judaism in AD 48. The other Queen (later Saint)
Helena was the mother of the Emperor Constantine, and a chapel in
the Holy Sepulchre consecrates the place where she found the remains
of the True Cross of Jesus.

James McDonald. Entrance to the
Church of the Virgin. 1864–5.
The Virgin Mary is also venerated by
Muslims who have a prayer niche here.
In addition there are Armenian, Greek
and Syrian Christian altars.

James McDonald. The Garden of Gethsemane and the Tomb of the Virgin in the Kedron Valley. 1864–5.
'Gethsemane' means an olive press, recalling the days when the mountain was covered with olive trees. The Tomb of the Virgin is the site of her presumed burial.

Zangaki. Garden of Gethsemane. c. 1880.
An unidentified person gave a batch of prints and negatives to a Sussex museum and this photograph was among them. They were then passed to the British Museum and from there to the PEF. It is very unusual to find negatives from this period.

James Graham. Garden of Gethsemane with Golden Gate in background. 1856. James Graham had an apartment in the tower of a building on the Mount of Olives. This is quite possibly his view.

James Graham. Kedron Valley. 1857. Showing the walls of Jerusalem and part of the village of Siloam.

Francis Bedford, No. 66. Village of Siloam. 1862.
Francis Bedford accompanied Edward, Prince of Wales on a tour of the Middle East following a plan originally devised by the late Prince Consort. This is one of the few photographs of the Arab village of Siloam taken from the Old City, the other side of the Kedron Valley.

James Graham. En Rogel, Ophel with Mount Moriah (the Dome of the Rock) from the south. c. *1853.*
Ophel is the possible site of David's city outside the Old City walls. En Rogel is the only permanently flowing spring near Jerusalem. It is also known as the Gihon Spring and the Fountain of the Virgin.

*Underwood and Underwood, No. 18. Jerusalem
from the Mount of Olives. c. 1900.*
This is half a stereo view and is part of a set 'Jerusalem
through the Stereoscope' issued with a booklet and a map
showing where the photographs were taken and giving the
field of view. Notable are the onion-shaped domes of the
Russian Church of Mary Magdalene built by the Czar in
1888 and therefore not in earlier photographs.

James Graham. Valleys of Hinnom and Kedron. c. 1853.
The ancient valleys of Hinnom (from the east) and Kedron (from the
north) meet here. The spring of En Rogel in the foreground is
obviously now well outside the Old City walls.

James Robertson and Felice Beato, No. 24.
The Pool of Siloam. 1857.
This is the 'New' Pool of Siloam, having been
created by King Hezekiah in 701 BC. The 'Old' Pool
of Siloam was the King's Pool, now called the Red
Pool, and is a vegetable garden. The 'New' Pool is
fed by the Fountain of the Virgin.

George Washington Wilson Company. Jacob's Well. c. *1890s.*
Shechem lying north of Jerusalem was an important city in
Palestine and is now called Nablus. Jacob's Well, also called the
Well of the Samaritan woman (John 4–5) is one of the few
undisputed sites in the life of Jesus.

James Robertson and Felice Beato, No. 26. The Well of Job. 1857.
Robertson describes the somewhat excessive ablutions, either for religion or cleanliness, that
took place at the Well of Job or Joab adding in the following, somewhat scathing, terms. ' ... a
more unwholesome mass of bigotry and dirt it would be impossible to imagine, and it appeared
as though a great and successful effort had been made to assemble all the scum of Christian Asia
into one spot for the especial profit of the Priests of the Holy Sepulchre'.

James Robertson and Felice Beato, No. 28. The Aceldama. 1857.
The Aceldama or 'The Field of Blood' was claimed to be the plot of land bought by
Judas with the thirty pieces of silver he received for betraying Jesus. It was a cursed place
and, from the time of the Crusades, was the burial ground for foreigners.

Frank Mason Good. 'The Hill of Evil Counsel'. 1875.
Overlooking 'The Field of Blood' is 'The Hill of Evil Counsel (or Council)'.
The photographer just describes it as this hill, but a contemporary writer has added
fancifully that the tree is the actual one on which Judas hanged himself (Matt. 27, 5).

James Robertson and Felice Beato. The Valley of Hinnom. 1857.
A rare photograph looking up the Hinnom Valley towards the Protestant Bishop
Gobat's School and the Tomb of David. The school, run by the London Missionary
Society, had about 40–50 boarders and also 20–30 day pupils. Later, a girl's school was
started and, like the boy's school, was also for Arab and Jewish pupils.

James McDonald. The Tomb of David. 1864–5.
According to tradition this was where King David was buried, though this has not been
established for certain as no supporting evidence has been found. It was also a Christian
shrine commemorating the Last Supper. The building became a Christian church, then
a Muslim shrine banned to Christians and finally a Jewish place of pilgrimage.

James Graham. Birket Mamillah. 1857.
Just south of the Jaffa Gate is the Birket Mamillah, a cistern for collecting valuable
rainwater. Until recent times, cisterns were an important part of the water supply: the
largest could hold millions of gallons.

The Walls of the City

Even the most modern maps clearly mark the walls of the Old City and show them to have changed little in recent centuries. However, the present walls are only some 400 years old, having been built by the Turkish Sultan Suleiman the Magnificent who ruled from 1520 to 1566. The main quest of many historians and archaeologists has been to locate the site of the walls at the time of Jesus and Herod. The PEF was, and still is, at the forefront of this search. There has also been a keen archaeological search for the walls of the City of Herod and the City of David. A tangled web of archaeological theory surrounds these explorations, sometimes involving no more than guesswork. A good guide through the maze is Kathleen Kenyon who was made a Dame for her work on the archaeology of Palestine and particularly Jerusalem. She was Director of the British School of Archaeology in Jerusalem from 1951–66 and directed the 1961–7 excavations that sought to discover the Old City walls. The PEF was a frequent partner for the British School of Archaeology, as were French and Canadian institutions. The story of the excavations is told in great detail in Kenyon's book *Digging Up Jerusalem*.

Herodian sites which the PEF suggested should be investigated are as follows: passages and vaults in the neighbourhood of the El Aksa Mosque; the Western Wall of the Haram; the area of the Ecce Homo Arch; the area between the Jaffa Gate and the Bab-es-Silsileh; the area of the Muristan and the Second Wall of Josephus; the area in front of the Damascus Gate; the Triple Gate; the Double Gate. Unfortunately not all could be investigated, for religious or political reasons. Permission to excavate needed to be sought from the Turkish Emperor. However, the permit (or firman) did not include the Dome of the Rock (the Haram esh-Sherif). Also, the Golden Gate of the Haram could only be approached by first sinking a shaft 81ft deep outside the Muslim burial ground and then tunnelling 143ft to reach the base of the wall.

For a photographic historian, Kenyon's work has the admirable virtue of summarizing the results of previous excavations. The photographs of Sergeant McDonald are the testimony of his work but Kathleen Kenyon also tells us what his Commanding Officer (Captain Charles Wilson) and his excavator (Lieutenant Charles Warren) were doing. In short, Wilson was making maps and plans of overground Jerusalem while Warren was exploring tunnels underneath David's city. The importance of both was immense. Wilson made the first accurate maps of Jerusalem and his bench marks are still visible today. Warren's excavations were not only the first but also they laid the foundations for all later work.

The first known settlement was south of the Old City of Herod. There is nothing to be seen on the surface now and, because of modern buildings, it is unlikely that much more will be discovered.

The Tomb of David on Mount Zion, although a place for worship, contains no evidence of his burial there, neither is there evidence of a tomb in the ancient City of David. It is possible that if he was buried in Jerusalem it is in one of the many unmarked tombs in the Kedron Valley. It is even more unlikely that there is any connection between David and David's Tower even though visitors are shown a room in which David is supposed to have composed the Psalms. The alternative name for the tower of the Citadel reflects the probability that this was fortified by King Herod on the north-eastern corner of the Ancient City Walls before the northern part of the Old City was built.

Even David's City was not built by David but by the Jebusites; Canaanites not Israelites. It was a small, walled city on the ridge of hills with the Pool of Siloam near its southern tip, the Kedron Valley on one side with the Tyropoeon Valley on the other. This latter valley was given its name (usually translated rather unhelpfully as 'the Cheese-makers') by Flavius Josephus, an historian who wrote *The Antiquities of the Jews* around AD 67–70. The Tyropoeon Valley that could be recognized then ran roughly north to south. It started at the Damascus Gate, passing along what is now El Wad Road near the Wailing Wall and then via the Dung Gate to join the Valley of Kedron on its east and the Valley of Hinnon on its west.

The Tyropoeon Valley of Josephus's time does not exist today. It was filled in with the rubble of successive metaphorical 'bulldozings' of the Ancient City: for example by Nebuchadnezzar (586 BC); the Persians (*c.* 350 BC); Ptolemy Soter (320 BC); Antiochus Epiphanes (168 BC); Pompey (63 BC); Herod (37 BC); Titus (AD 70); Hadrian (AD 132); the Persians again (AD 614) and the Mongols (AD 1244).

Each of these conquerors destroyed most of the city as it stood in their time. It was only after all this destruction, that Suleiman the Magnificent built the walls that today encompass the Old City. The depth of rubble in some places is extraordinary. Lieutenant Warren, excavating in this area in 1869, had to sink a shaft down 81ft to get below the rubble.

Even away from the Tyropoeon Valley, Mrs Finn reported that when the Reverend John Nicolayson, a missionary, was supervising the digging of foundations of the Protestant Church, they had to dig down through 40ft of rubble to reach solid rock. The Missionary School was outside the Zion Gate but when the new dining hall was being built in 1910, the headmaster Charles Hornstein discovered a Roman mosaic 6ft down and a second beneath this, 19ft below the surface.

As well as rubble from past cities there was also much more recent detritus. Black's *Guide* of 1912 is typically uncompromising:

'The streets are not drained – few are wide enough for wheeled traffic. Attempts at sanitation are of the most primitive order ... It is highly advisable to walk very discreetly through the narrow malodorous alleys and lanes filled with garbage, which is removed at long intervals in baskets slung on donkeys.'

Even if the Tyropoeon Valley and the City of David have been buried under rubble, the surviving remnant, the Pool of Siloam and its source the Spring Gihon (also known as the Well or Fountain of the Virgin), have their place in biblical history. King David's defeat of the Jebusites is recorded in 2 Samuel 1: 31, which describes how Job or Joab, son of Zeruiah, went up the tunnel from the spring and suprised the defenders so that the Israelites under David could take the fortress.

The most famous Herodian wall is the Wailing Wall. This is not a city wall, but rather the only fragment of the Herodian temple to survive the Roman destruction in AD 70.

David himself spent so much time on campaigns consolidating his empire that he did little for Jerusalem itself. His son Solomon started a building programme with the first temple built on the threshing floor of Araunah the Jebusite. His palace and other buildings seem to have been south of the temple and north of David's City. Solomon died in 926–925 BC and Herod's Temple was not started until about 20 BC. The events in between, including the destruction of the City and the capture of the people, are unfortunately no part of photographic history, for no trace of the walls survived above ground. Even the experts cannot agree on exactly where the walls were, but by Herod's time the Antonia Fortress and the Citadel, built on earlier foundations, were the key points. The wall between them is the most important factor because most interpretations would put Golgotha, and therefore the place of the Holy Sepulchre, outside the City walls; Christ as a Jew would not have been buried inside the city walls.

Frank Mason Good. 1866.
Published by Francis Frith 1876.
Peasants of Jerusalem.

Charles A. Hornstein. Shepherd carrying lamb. c. *1890.*
Another example of Hornstein's rapport with his photographic
subjects, who were otherwise unrecorded at this time. It is
perhaps worth noting that Charles's father and uncle were both
hotel-keepers requiring a regular supply of meat.

Charles A. Hornstein. Man with gun. c. *1890.*
The Mission School where Hornstein was headmaster
also taught Arab and Jewish children. The natural and
easy pose could lead one to speculate that the armed
man was a parent of one Hornstein's pupils.

American Colony Photograper, No. 186. The Citadel of Zion. c. *1905.*
This is now part of El Qal'a, the citadel together with David's Tower by the Jaffa Gate.

Zangaki, No. 1144. The Jaffa Gate. c. *1900.*
The photographer took many views over the years, updating them only when changes
made it necessary. Sometimes the considerations were commercial. The sign in the
upper right of the photograph has been blackened out on the negative. In a similar view,
no. 1039, the name on the left has been obliterated, possibly because they stocked rival
photographs. The distant view is of the windmill, built by Sir Moses Montefiore in 1858.

American Colony Photographer, No. 332. Breach in city wall at Jaffa Gate. c. *1901.*
Turkey, the so-called 'Sick Man of Europe' was sought after by the other nations of Europe. Jerusalem
became the battleground with most countries already represented through their churches. Germany,
searching for a place in the sun, wanted more so Kaiser Wilhelm II came ostentatiously to lay the foundation
stone of the Abbey Church. To do this, he wished to ride into the Holy City on a white horse and, as the
existing gates were not tall enough, a passage was made through the wall next to the Jaffa Gate. Also visible
looking into the city is the shop of Vester, the main outlet for the American Colony group of photographers,
and the Grand New Hotel which rivalled the nearby Mediterranean Hotel.

James Robertson and Felice Beato, No. 13. The Sion [Zion] Gate. 1857.
The Damascus Gate is the northern gate; the Zion Gate the southern leading to Mount Zion, the supposed
site of the Tomb of David and the scene of the Last Supper. Robertson comments on the huts of the lepers
just inside the gate and unsympathetically on their freedom to beg all over Jerusalem.

James Robertson and Felice Beato. The Damascus Gate. 1857.
The distance to Damascus is 180 miles but for centuries it was the road travelled by government
officials. Robertson said that the Damascus Gate is the start of a pleasant promenade on the top
of the walls of the city, 'It is easy and safe … even for the most nervous people.'

*James Graham. The Huldah Gate, the Double Gate
in the El Aksa Mosque. 1855–8.*
This is not a city gate but a sealed pair of gates that had provided
entrance to the Mosque for Pilgrims. Inside, the flight of steps
are of unequal size to concentrate the pilgrims' thoughts.

James Graham. The Golden Gate. 1855–8.
The double gate is also called the Gates of Mercy and both Jews and
Christians believe that when the Messiah comes he will enter Jerusalem
through these gates. This is also the gate through which Jesus rode on
Palm Sunday. Muslims believe that the gate will be opened on Judgement
Day and that they will pass through it to Paradise.

James Graham. The Golden Gate from the west within the Holy Place. 1855–8.
Until the Sultan ordered the Pasha to escort the Duke and Duchess of Brabant round the Holy Place (the Temple Mount) at Easter 1855, it had been closed to non-Muslims and any infidel setting foot inside risked their life. This must be one of the earliest photographs taken inside the Temple Mount. It became easier to visit as the years progressed.

Anon, from Mrs Dauglish's collection. The Golden Gate. c. 1904.
Mrs Dauglish gave lantern slide lectures on the Holy Land to such institutions as the Temperance Clubs. This is probably one of her own slides, but others identified were from pictures taken by the George Washington Wilson company, Frances Frith and Frank Mason Good. Some one hundred slides were in use for thirty or forty years.

James McDonald. The Ecce Homo Arch. 1864.
This is the most photographed part of the Via Dolorosa, although it is not a Station of
the Cross. It is traditionally the spot where Pontius Pilate said 'Behold the Man', before
handing Jesus over to the rabbis. This is one of the very few photographs taken before
the Convent of the French Sisters of Zion was built on the right.

Bonfils. Camels in the desert. c. *1905.*
The photograph was coloured by Photoglob in Zurich; the original sepia
photograph had almost certainly been made by the Bonfils family of
Beirut twenty years earlier. Even though it is quite possible that the
photograph was staged, it still has an air of authenticity.

Bonfils. Bedouin nomads in front of their tent. c. *1905.*
Perhaps of the same origins as the previous picture, although its
authenticity is more credible. Since the time of Egyptian rule of the Holy
Land attempts had been made to force Bedouins into villages, although
such efforts were largely unsuccessful.

Anon. Bedouin peasants at the well. c. *1905.*
Another timeless photograph. The well was the social centre of Arab
women's life, whether Bedouin or farming peasant.

Photoglob, Zurich. The Tower of David, the Turkish Citadel. c. 1905
from an earlier negative.
The present Tower of David was built by Suleiman the Magnificent around 1537. The
lower stones of the towers are Herodian and so are the same age as the Wailing Wall.
In Herod's time, the tower on the right, now called after King David, was known as
Phasael, whilst the tower on the left was known as Hippicus: and both formed part of
Herod's palace. There is no connection with King David.

Photoglob, Zurich, PZ 15008. The Jaffa Gate. c. *1905 from an earlier negative.*
As Jerusalem expanded, the easiest direction for this was on the level ground to the east along the
Jaffa Road. Just inside the gate was the British Consulate, the British Church, Moses Hornstein's
Mediterranean Hotel – the best in its time – and the Thomas Cook office.

Photoglob, Zurich, PZ 15010. The market inside the Jaffa Gate. c. *1900.*
The main route into Jerusalem was from Jaffa, so urban development and the local market were concentrated in this area.

Anon, from Mrs Dauglish's collection. The First Station of the
Cross and the Tower of Antonia. c. *1904.*
According to tradition, the courtroom of Pontius Pilate was located
here and it was from here that Jesus was condemned to death, the
event of the First Station of the Cross. Herod the Great established a
fortress here named in honour of the emperor Mark Antony.
Previously the Maccabean fortress Baris had been on the site.

The Holy Sepulchre and Via Dolorosa

For Christians of all denominations the most holy site is the Holy Sepulchre, the ground on which Jesus was crucified, was buried and rose from the dead, though archaeologists and theologians may argue whether the present Church of the Holy Sepulchre is on the exact site or even near it. The present church is based on the Crusader church of the twelfth century. The first church on the site was built by the Emperor Constantine and dedicated on 17 September 335 on what had been the site of the Temple of Venus, built by his mother Queen Helena. This magnificent church was destroyed by the Persians three centuries later. Modestus, the Abbot of St Theodosius, restored much of the church and the church described by the pilgrim Arnulf in 680 is the Constantine church as restored by Modestus. An earthquake, probably that of 808, caused damage to the church but repairs were carried out in 815 by the Patriarch Thomas.

The church had been razed to the ground in 1009 and then rebuilt between 1037 and 1047 by the Crusaders. The situation between the various religious groups in the period thereafter is a tangled weave of religious and political intrigue. Eventually the Turkish Sultan and the Jerusalem Pasha issued *status quo* ordinances confirming the edict first made by Sultan Osman III in 1757.

The Crusader church was divided among the seven sects identified below. The first accurate plan of the church was made in 1865 by the British Ordnance Survey team of Royal Engineers led by Captain Charles Wilson and marks the various chapels within the church. The chapels are mainly Greek Orthodox but there are also Latin (Roman Catholic), Coptic, Armenian, Syrian (Aramaic), Ethiopian (Abyssinian) and Arabic Orthodox chapels. The area in the centre of the church, Calvary in the Latin tradition and Golgotha in the Greek, is keenly disputed between the different sects so detailed rules and rituals had to be enforced to prevent bickering. The *status quo* had the curious result that all photographs of the entrance to the Church show a ladder above the door. Over the years the actual ladder has been renewed but it remains in the same place because the different sects could not agree on who should move it! There are countless other stories of petty rivalries but the final irony is that the keys of the whole church were entrusted before the *status quo* ordinance to a Muslim caretaker who still opens and closes the church.

The traditional approach to the church, particularly at Easter, is the Way of Sorrows, otherwise called the Way of the Cross but almost universally known as the Via Dolorosa. This was the path followed by Jesus on his way to his cruci-fixion and is marked at intervals by the Stations of the Cross. Churches throughout the world have a series of tablets or plaques at intervals round their walls usually representing twelve stations to remind Christians of the crucifixion and resurrection and to provide a focal point for prayer. In some churches, mostly Protestant, there are only eleven stations as the sixth is contentious. It is supposed to be the spot where St Veronica mopped the brow of Christ, leaving the imprint of his features on the cloth. This event was not mentioned in the Bible and in fact seems to have not been mentioned at all until about the eighth century. Because of this, some Christians are unwilling to give this station equality with biblical events.

The Via Dolorosa begins inside St Stephen's Gate on the north side of the Temple Mount, near the Antonia Fortress.

The Stations of the Cross in Jerusalem differ from those in most churches. Stations 13, 14 and 15 are Crusader sites within the Church of the Holy Sepulchre itself. The stations are as follows:

1   Jesus is condemned (Matthew 27: 24–26).
2   Jesus is made to carry his cross (Mark 15: 20). Between this station and the next is the Ecce Homo Arch where Pontius Pilate uttered the words 'Behold the Man' and abandoned Christ (John 19: 7–8).
3   Jesus falls the first time (Hebrews 2: 6–9).
4   Jesus meets his mother (Luke 2: 34–35).
5   Simon of Cyrene takes up the cross (Mark 15: 21).
6   Veronica wipes the face of Jesus.

7   Jesus falls a second time (Isaiah 53: 5).
8   Jesus speaks to the women (Luke 23: 27–31).
9   Jesus falls a third time (Isaiah 53: 6).
10 Jesus is stripped of his garments (John 19: 23–24).
11 Jesus is nailed to the cross (Mark 15: 22).
12 Jesus dies on the cross (John 19: 30).
13 Jesus is taken down from the cross (Luke 23: 50–53).
14 Jesus is laid in the sepulchre (John 19: 41).
15 Jesus rises from the dead (Mark 16: 1–11).

It is important to realise that nowadays the Stations of the Cross are devotional not historical. The actual path that Jesus trod is buried under 60–70 feet of rubble and there is no guarantee that roads built later were built over the original roads. Likewise, it is impossible to pinpoint the location of many of the stations; Veronica's station is not the only one that is not specifically set out in the Gospels. However to insist on geographical or historical accuracy is to miss the point.

The later stations are set within the Church of the Holy Sepulchre. The Reverend G. Robinson Lees BA, FRGS was the headmaster of the Protestant Missionary School in the 1890s and a keen photographer. In his book *Pictorial Palestine* he gives a fairly scathing view of the Holy Sepulchre at the time: 'Nowhere in all the world is blind superstitious folly and sectarian hatred so diligently engaged in distorting the truth of Christ's teaching. How can anyone possibly believe that all that is degrading, disgusting and untrue should be associated with the last resting place of the Saviour of Mankind?' He continues in this vein for another seven pages! It seems that Protestants, not represented in the Holy Sepulchre, often preferred the Garden Tomb of Gordon's Calvary as the resting place in spite of its dubious authenticity due to Gordon's misunderstanding of the route of the north city wall in Herodian times.

Looking back one hundred years or more we may wonder why, in the face of such disillusionment, anyone wanted to go to the Holy Land. But the lure of the Holy Land for nineteenth-century visitors was summed up by Florence Barclay, a writer of "wholesome fiction". Her novel *The Rosary* sold over one million copies. In 1881 she married her father's curate in Limehouse and as an eighteen-year-old set out for her honeymoon in Palestine. Her daughter wrote in a biography based on her diary and letters home, that

'Her spirit of pilgrimage was a very living thing; it was what one might call the spirit of historical realism in religion. She wanted intensely to go to Palestine because it was in Palestine that God became man. She wanted to walk the roads that He had walked, to climb the same mountains and pray on them too; to feel her eyes were resting upon the same scene of blue waters and hills and nestling white villages that the eyes of Christ beheld. She wanted Jerusalem, Bethlehem, Nazareth, Jericho to become real places to her, instead of mere names and dream-cities of the imagination. To her they were the scenes of the greatest drama in history. She had always loved them, and from her babyhood's days had lived in them in loving fancy. At last she was to *see* them, and the sense of worship in her responded with a deep joy and wondering awe.'

American Colony Photographer. The Via Dolorosa. c. *1900.* This view was one of the most popular with tourists and pilgrims who were probably convinced of its authenticity. The actual street level at the time of Jesus was anything from 40 to 80 feet lower. The present buildings were built on the rubble, and the route and stations were decided in the fifteenth century by the Franciscan monks of the nearby Monastery of the Flagellation.

Bonfils. The Second Station of the Cross. c. *1870.*
The nearby Monastery of the Flagellation and the Chapel of
Condemnation mark the place where Jesus was scourged and the crown
of thorns placed on his head.

James Robertson and Felice Beato. The Ecce Homo Arch. 1857–8.
In this photograph the arch and wall seen in the McDonald photograph (p. 48) are
now shown from the other side. Unfortunately for the tradition that claims it was
from here that Pontius Pilate cried out 'Ecce Homo' (Behold the Man), it seems
that the arch was probably built as a three-part Triumphal Arch for the emperor
Hadrian, who ruled from 117 to 138.

Bonfils, No. 263. The Fourth Station and the House of the Wicked Rich Man. c. *1870.*
The parable of the poor man Lazarus who went to Heaven and the rich man who went to Hell
(Luke 16: 19–31) was the subject of many a sermon in Victorian times. The nearby Armenian
Catholic church of Our Lady of the Spasm contains a sixth-century mosaic of her footprints.

Bonfils, No. 264. The Fifth Station: Simon of Cyrene
made to carry the cross. c. *1870*
No one has really explained why at this spot the Roman
soldiers ordered a visitor from the country, Simon of
Cyrene, to carry the cross for Jesus (Mark 15: 21).

Underwood and Underwood. Pilgrims on the Via Dolorosa. 1897.
Improvements in photographic technology meant that, by the turn of the century, the people as well as the places could be represented.

Underwood and Underwood.
Easter procession of the Greek Patriarch. 1903.
In spite of the efforts of the Czar, the Greek (i.e. not the Russian) Orthodox Church controlled some seventy per cent of the Holy Sepulchre. At Easter around 20,000 pilgrims flooded into Jerusalem. Nearly all slept in dormitories in a state of poverty.

American Colony Photographer.
The Sixth Station. c. 1900.
Tradition has it that here Veronica wiped the face of Jesus and the image of his face appeared on the cloth. The cloth is now in St Peter's Basilica in Rome but does not seem to have been tested in the same way as the Turin Shroud. The incident does not appear in the Bible and indeed is not recorded anywhere until the twelfth century. Photograph reproduced courtesy of Agnes Rammant Collection, Belgium.

Dr Conrad Schick. Holy Sepulchre, Old Dome. c. *1861–7.*
One of the initial conflicts leading to the Crimean War was the Czar's attempt (on behalf of the Russian Orthodox Church)
to take over authority for the Holy Places, not only from the Greek Orthodox Church but from "The Latins", the French-led
Roman Catholics. The *status quo* from the Turkish Sultan did not solve the problem of responsibility; eventually the roof of
the Holy Sepulchre fell into a state of serious disrepair and no one could agree who should repair it.

Bonfils, No. 848. Stairway to the Holy Sepulchre. c. *1880.*
Black's *Guide to Jerusalem* of 1912 writes 'At the very gate of the Church a painfully
incongruous note is struck by the yelling and screams of the dealers in "articles de
piété" – fit descendants of those who made the Temple a "house of merchandise."'

Dr Conrad Schick. Holy Sepulchre: The New Dome. c. 1869.
The French claim to sole authority was based on a treaty of 1535. The Russian Czar
based his on a seventh-century treaty. To thwart these geo-political pressures, in 1853
the Sultan offered to fund the repairs out of his own pocket. In fact, repairs did not start
until March 1867 and were eventually financed by all three groups.

Bonfils, No. 1209. Greek washing of the feet. c. 1885.
On the eve of the Passover Jesus washed the feet of his disciples (John 13: 1–16) as an act of humility. In the Greek Orthodox Easter ritual
there is a huge ceremony when the Greek Patriarch symbolically washes the feet of ordinary worshippers.

Underwood and Underwood. The Church of the Holy Sepulchre. 1897.
This viewpoint of the Church façade must have appeared in every collection of Jerusalem photographs. The innocuous-looking ladder has a bloody history. Inside the church are thirty-seven Holy Places, each of which were fiercely protected. Arguments about exact demarcation lines led to fighting, sometimes with fatal results. In 1855 the Turkish rulers reaffirmed and enforced the *status quo* that in theory ended the disputes. However, in this photograph it is possible to see that the ladder remains against the window with no one willing or able to remove it.

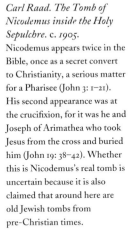

Carl Raad. The Tomb of Nicodemus inside the Holy Sepulchre. c. 1905.
Nicodemus appears twice in the Bible, once as a secret convert to Christianity, a serious matter for a Pharisee (John 3: 1–21). His second appearance was at the crucifixion, for it was he and Joseph of Arimathea who took Jesus from the cross and buried him (John 19: 38–42). Whether this is Nicodemus's real tomb is uncertain because it is also claimed that around here are old Jewish tombs from pre-Christian times.

Photoglob, Zurich, PZ 15014. Calvary or Golgotha. c. 1890.
The Twelfth Station of the Cross is the Greek Orthodox chapel above the Calvary rock on which Jesus's cross was erected.

Zangaki, No. 1175. The Chapel of the Angel. c. *1885.*
Part of the actual Holy Sepulchre or burial place is the Fourteenth Station of the Cross; this is
the site of the tomb that Mary Magdalene found empty on the Sunday after the crucifixion.

Zangaki, No. 1236. The Fifteenth Station of the Cross: the Chapel of Saint Helena. c. 1885.
Normally there are only twelve Stations of the Cross but in Jerusalem there are fifteen (not all of them universally recognized).
In 326 Queen Helena, the mother of the Christian Emperor Constantine, discovered a crypt containing three crosses. It is claimed
that the supposed cross of Christ restored the health of a woman with an incurable disease.

The Dome of the Rock

Mount Moriah is one of the most holy sites in the world for Muslims, Jews and Christians. It is known by a number of different names including the Dome of the Rock, Qubbat es Sakhra and the Temple Mount. Older books refer to the Dome of the Rock as the Mosque of Omar, but it never was a mosque. It was, however a very holy site for Muslims, third only to Mecca and Medina. It was here that the Prophet Muhammad traditionally landed after his flight through the Seven Heavens on his Wonder Horse el-Burak. This was the furthest point of the Muslim world at that time and hence it is called El Aksa. The El Aksa Mosque forms part of the site but is in a quite different part. In fact, even the El Aksa Mosque was not originally built as a mosque but as a Christian church for Justinian and was the headquarters of the Crusaders. Also on this site,

Photoglob, Zurich. Interior of the Mosque of Omar. c. 1905.
Technically the original title is incorrect as this was not a mosque nor built by Omar, but rather was built by Caliph Abd al-Malik
in AD 691. The Dome is over the Rock (seen here) on which Muhammad is believed to have returned to earth.

buried under the rubble of centuries, is what remains of the Temple of Solomon, though the Wailing Wall or Western Wall of the Temple is still visible. Traditionally, the story of the Dome of the Rock began when King David erected an altar on the threshing floor of Ophel the Jebusite, on the hill to the north of what was then the City of David. This was followed by the Temple of Solomon and, around 20 BC, by the magnificent Temple of Herod. For Jews, Mount Moriah became the Temple Mount.

Jewish tradition holds that the Ark of the Covenant is buried here, and Jews themselves would not set foot on Mount Moriah even if allowed to. Christians had no such reservations but were denied entry by Muslims.

In his memoirs *Stirring Times* the British Consul James Finn gives a very good account of the Dome of the Rock from the perspective of a nineteenth-century outsider being given special permission to enter.

The times were exceptional for it was during the Crimean War. At the end of March 1854 Britain and France had declared war on Russia, in defence of Turkey. In mid-September 1854 the Siege of Sebastapol had begun and, though the siege was to last for a year and ultimately end favourably for the Alliance, at Easter 1855 the situation was critical and there were even rumours of a Russian victory. The Turkish Sultan therefore had very good reason to issue a permit to the Duke and Duchess of Brabant to visit the Dome of the

Photoglob, Zurich, from an earlier Bonfils, PZ 15018. Place du Temple du Solomon. c. 1895.
The Crimean War (1854–7) had opened the gates of the Temple Mount but penetration by photographers was slow and gradual. However the tourist pilgrim with spending money was becoming increasingly important for the prosperity of the city.

James McDonald. Eastern View of the platform [Temple Mount] from the Golden Gate. 1864–5.
As a member of the Survey party trained in the use of theodolites etc. McDonald would have had no problem matching
the sections of a panorama. This one in particular captures the grandeur of the holy site from the outside.

Rock. The Duke of Brabant, a Roman Catholic, later became King Leopold II of Belgium. The Duchess was a princess of the Austrian royal house and especially welcome as Austria had not supported Russia against Turkey, as the Czar had expected.

The Turkish Sultan placed a huge burden on the shoulders of the Jerusalem Pasha who had been appointed Governor of Jerusalem only six weeks earlier. Not only did he have to please the royal guests but also he had to prevent any dissension between the other diplomats. Whatever the political background, Finn's memoirs provide a very good description of the places within the Dome of the Rock in the middle of the last century. Here follows an extract from them:

[One of the most important] events in connection with this Royal visit was the entrance to the Hharam (Noble Sanctuary of the Moslems, Temple Enclosure of the Jews on Mount Moriah), for which unprecedented privilege His Royal Highness was bearer of a special Firmân from the Sultan.

I say unprecedented, because although private individuals had before then gained stealthy admission in disguise, or by night, […] this was to be a public and daylight entry. And it was understood that a select number would be admitted in the company or train of the Royal persons thus specially privileged.

The signal honour thus accorded by the Sultan to the Duke and Duchess of Brabant was consistent with the line adopted throughout, according to which these

were treated as representative personages from the Latin Allies of [Turkey]; though Belgium was not in the alliance, she was of the same religion, and this was quite enough for the Oriental view of the situation. [...]

The Sanctuary of the Hharam had been always hitherto, while under Mohammedan rule, an interdicted place to non-believers (hence its name Hharam, sanctuary, 'set apart'). The line of apartments along the inner side of the western wall and cloister of the great enclosure (which it will be remembered is a vast quadrangle covering all the summit of Mount Moriah) was allotted to learned religious students or professors, and the whole enclosure was guarded by a police of African race, called Takuri. [...] The appearance of these men was calculated to inspire fear. They were above middle height, active, and powerfully built; black in colour, but many of them good-looking, save when fanatic fury distorted their countenances; then indeed they were terrible to behold, and still more terrible to encounter, for they were armed with huge clubs which they were ever ready to use in defence of the inviolability of the Sanctuary. More than one serious case had occurred in which these Africans had all but murdered Christian trespassers into the Hharam, and it was dangerous even to approach the gates or to be seen upon the city walls too near this forbidden paradise. [...]

The Pashà had to deal with these men, before any safe entrance could be assured to the Royal party. [...]

The regiment forming the Jerusalem garrison was chiefly Turkish, and therefore to be depended upon by the Pashà in his arrangements for the safety of the guests entrusted to him by his Sovereign. But it was a critical matter to obey the Sultan's Firmân and to risk admitting Christians into the Sanctuary […]

Everyone who heard anything of the grand opportunity so long hoped for, even against hope, by the old residents of Jerusalem, who had for years looked down with longing upon the glorious Temple Court from Olivet or from the site of Antonia at the governor's house – everybody was on the *qui vive*, whether residents or travellers. But the thing was to be kept as quiet as possible. […] Still the excitement was great. […]

His Excellency had expressed his positive desire that neither pilgrims (as distinguished from travellers), nor ordinary residents of the city were to be privileged on the occasion. Pilgrims alone would have furnished a host unmanageably large, and enough to exasperate the Moslems.

Those of the ordinary residents who besieged the English Consulate went down to the Seraglio, followed by equally eager travellers, to wait and see whether the authorities would grant them admission.

As it was known to many of the candidates for admission, that even Moslems are not suffered to enter the sanctuaries in their street shoes, but must either walk without any, or put on fresh morocco slippers carried thither by servants on purpose, it was wonderful to find what a prodigious demand was now made all of a sudden in the bazaars for the yellow slippers called *alasheen*: such a purchase cannot often have been made in one day at Jerusalem.

But even now the general Moslem population had no knowledge of what was preparing to be done. The Pashà had kept his own counsel; and as the time drew near, he quietly posted guards of soldiers at the various gates to keep out the Moslems, who might have given trouble. He had purposely chosen an hour in the after-noon when prayers would not be going on, and when there would probably be very few Moslems in the Sacred Enclosure. […]

But people were too eager to be prudent; long pent-up desire to set foot upon the Temple Mountain, to walk within its glorious courts, burst over and beyond all bounds of restraint; and the great crowd of travellers, most of whom never expected to be in the Holy Land again in their lives, brought an unexpected difficulty into the case. They had no idea of prudent reserve, had no knowledge of the real danger of the thing, did not see that the admission of Christians to St. Sophia – formerly a Byzantine church, and now nothing more than the grand mosque of the Turkish capital – had no real parallel with the throwing open to unbelievers of the spot in the world most scared to the Moslems, after, and perhaps not even after, the Kaaba sanctuary at Mecca.

It is not only that Moslems believe the Jerusalem Hharam to be identical with the precincts and the site of Solomon's Temple, and therefore holy; but they believe Abraham, David, and Elijah to have worshipped there, and all the most miraculous part of the history of their own prophet Mohammed is linked with the Sacred Rock, whence he is declared to have ascended to heaven on the midnight journey, when the horse Borak carried him up to receive divine revelations of the religion of Islam.

Nothing can exceed the genuine earnest reverence of devout Moslems for this spot, connected not only with the past, but with the future triumphs of Islâm, when Mohammed and 'Our Lord Jesus' shall come to judgement.

The very place where Mohammed shall then sit is shown on a pillar which projects from the Hharam Wall, over the Valley of Jehoshaphat. And over the same valley will, they believe, be stretched that slender bridge over which the faithful will cross on their way to eternal bliss. This Sanctuary is, indeed, as they call it, the Hharam esh Sherref – the Honourable (or Noble) Sanctuary. [...]

And within this shrine Moslems had told us a part of the foundations of Solomon's Temple was visible: and the Jews had told us that there was the Stone of Foundation upon which the Temple had stood; and upon which, according to some, the High Priest had habitually sprinkled the blood in the Second Temple, where the Ark of the Covenant and the Mercy Seat (never seen since the destruction by Nebuchanezzar, but believed by the Jews to be still within the precincts) were awanting.

We were at last then to enter the courts which most Jews would refuse to walk over (even if allowed by Moslems), lest they should be guilty of disrespect to the holy law of God, which they believe that their priests in ancient time hid away beneath the pavement in some of the many subterranean treasure-houses, hewn out by Solomon in the mountain; those courts erewhile thronged by joyful worshippers, even in the days when our Saviour went thither to teach, to heal, and Himself to fulfil the law.

Those courts now calm and lovely, if comparatively deserted, in which the most devout, the bravest, the most fanatically zealous of the Jewish people had perished, which had been so polluted with human bodies and human blood that never again could Jewish priests offer sacrifice, or Jewish people worship there, until the Mosaic purifications with the ashes of the red heifer shall have been accomplished. [...]

We were to approach the spot where the threshing floor of Araunah [Ornan] the Jebusite had been, the site of King David's altar; the site of Abraham's altar on Moriah; the site of the Holy of Holies, the earthly throne of Divine majesty and presence, the spot where the Veil had been rent in twain! There was not much room left in our minds for dwelling upon possible dangers. [...]

We went down on our way to the Seraglio, where all were to assemble. In the *Via Dolorosa* the Prussian, the American and the English Consular parties met together. At the Seraglio the kawwâsses [household officials] had to push our way through a multitude of eager expectants (a good proportion of whom were English travellers) who were assembled in the Pashà's residence. [...] Here the Turkish secretary distributed to the consular parties, and to them only, tickets for admission.

Scarcely was this finished when it was announced that their Royal Highnesses, who had met the Pashà and the military authorities in another apartment, had already entered the sacred precincts, and we were to follow at once – which we accordingly did, [...] passing through a narrow dark passage, which forms the private entrance to the Sanctuary precincts from the Pashà's Seraglio. It was speedily found that the tickets were of no use, for the crowd in our rear pushed us forward and defied all attempts to exclude them: in they rushed like a flood. [...]

It was some time before anyone could recover anything like the reverential feelings due to the solemnity of the place we were entering: religious meditation was at that moment out of the question. All of a sudden we emerged into daylight and bright sunshine; and we stood within the Sanctuary on the smooth scarped rock cut away some thousand years ago. Here the main body of the Turkish garrison awaited the company. The soldiers were fully armed, and closed around us as we followed the Pashà, who, with the officers in command, led the Royal visitors forward.

We then crossed the general space of the vast enclosure towards the centre, where are the steps by which the upper platform and the shrine (the Dome of the Rock) is reached. At the foot of the steps we were stopped to 'put off our shoes from off our feet.' Ascending upon the wide platform by those steps, we were now on a level with the grand edifice commonly and erroneously called by Europeans the 'Mosque of Omar,' but by the Mohammedans 'Dome of the Rock' – seeing that this building, with all its magnificence, is but a cover for protection of the Holy Sakhrah, and of a few traditional adjuncts which were gathered round it.

We entered this central shrine.

To our great surprise, there, enclosed by a railing, was a huge mass of primeval rock lying beneath the Great Dome; a rich canopy of green silk and gold hanging over it.

Astonishment and awe at seeing this rock above the floor – grey, rugged, and immense – took possession of our mind, even before the sensation of admiration for its shrine, with the rich colours of the stained glass windows, the gorgeous silk canopy, the profuse gilding of the interior, the arabesques, the mosaics, the costly marble pillars.

This then was the 'Foundation of the House of God' of which the Moslems had formerly told us – the 'Stone of Foundation' the Jews had talked about, as visible within the Sanctuary – yet no mere *stone*, but the vast rocky apex of the Holy Mountain itself. Truly this was the 'top of the Mountain' on which Josephus tells us the Temple stood. There is no spot so high as this culminating point beneath the dome.

And the rough unhewn simplicity amidst all the splendour of the shrine! Ah! that spoke of reverent obedience to the Law given by Moses (Exodus xx.25), forbidding any altar to be built up of hewn stone, 'for if thou lift up thy tool upon it thou hast polluted it.'

And if King Solomon in his scrupulous obedience to this command had caused even the stones of which the outer works of the Temple and its courts were built, to be carved and finished before they were brought to the Holy Mountain, so that 'no sound of axe or hammer was heard' during all the progress of the building, here before our eyes lay the evidence in all its rugged majesty that the rock which had served as the Altar base to King David, when God answered him by fire from heaven – and earlier still to Abraham, when he was prepared to offer his son – that Rock thus consecrated had been left intact and unhewn; no tool had been raised upon it to pollute it, by Israelite, or by Moslem.

The first glance at the rough rock made clear, as in an instant by a flash of vivid light, where those Altars, and the Holy of Holies must have stood; there and nowhere else – so it seemed to us them – so it has seemed to us from that day forward – had been their fitting and 'Majestic site'. [...]

The Pashà was leading the way with the Royal party, and he was attended by Shaikh Mohammed Danaf, well known to us as the hereditary guardian of the Sanctuary. The Africans, mentioned above, are the *guards*; but Shaikh Mohammed Danaf held an office corresponding to that of Dean in an English Cathedral. [...] A liberal present had reconciled Shaikh Mohammed to the Christian visit to the Sanctuary. [...]

The young Danaf guardians showed me where a large piece of the rock had been cut off 'by Nebuchadnezzar', whereas the great mass of the rock is in its primitive original condition of unhewn ruggedness. But history tells us that it was the Crusaders who cut away a portion of the rock, in order that they might fit their altars upon it.

They also pointed out the footprint of the creature 'Borak', upon which Mohammed ascended to the seventh heaven attended by the angel Gabriel, and a variety of other legendary matter connected with the Prophet and with the rock. [...]

Having passed round the great Rock, we went to the steps, which at the south-east side lead down into the natural hollow or cave in the Rock. [...]

We gazed round at the harmony of the proportions of the building, at the rich gold-fretted work, the mosaics; the beautiful stained-glass windows, lovely beyond description. We could not on this occasion understand what it was that gave the rich brilliancy, as of jewels, to the coloured light; but long afterwards we discovered that this was produced by an ingenious mode of setting each portion of glass so as to obtain a variety of reflected light within the windows. We looked at the *verde antique* and other marbles, the double columns, and those in the midst; at the Solemn Rock where, they told us again, the 'House of God' had been.

We went down the steps into the cave, the Rock being visible overhead. There our Moslem friends pointed out around the sides of the Cave the praying stations (Makâm) of Abraham, David, Solomon, and Elijah.

But this Cave (so evidently natural, one of the ordinary hollows that abound in the limestone rocks of this country), surely it was the hiding place to which allusion is made in the history of King David's Sacrifice (I Chron. xxii. 20). Ornan and his sons had been threshing wheat upon their threshing-floor; they saw the angel, feared and hid themselves, where? but in the cavern beside their threshing-floor, which was also no doubt their granary for the winnowed grain.

There above their heads was the hole in the rock roof of the Cave through which the grain would have been poured down from above, and which in early ages gave this rock its name of 'Lapis pertusus.' [...]

Our Moslem guides struck the centre of the floor in the Cave, to convince us that there is a large cavity below. This (lower depth) they call the Beer el Arruâhh, the pit where departed Souls dwell waiting for the resurrection. The instant thought on hearing this strange Moslem legend was of the verse in the vi chapter of Revelations, about the souls of them that were slain for the Word of God, waiting 'under the altar.' [...]

Here was evidently an opening to those treasure chambers hewn out in the solid rock below, of which we had read and heard from the Jews, and in one of which they believe the Ark of the Covenant to have been secreted by the priests, under advice from the Prophet Jeremiah, before Nebuchadnezzar captured the city and broke into the Sanctuary. [...]

The Pashà and the royal party were moving rapidly on and we followed. Mounting again we issued from the Dome of the Rock at the Southern Portal. We went across the great platform, descending the flight of steps on that side, and went towards the Mosque of 'Aksa (a real *Mosque, i.e.* a building within which Moslems assemble for public worship; the Dome of the Rock is only a Shrine, or Sanctuary, used for special prayers and ceremonials).

We passed through an avenue of trees. They told us that the great cypresses had been planted by Nebuchadnezzar, and an ancient olive by the Prophet Mohammed. Near the entrance of the Mosque is a spot where, they told us, the sons of Aaron (Neby Haroon) are buried.

The vastness of the edifice struck us as we entered and passed along its length (southwards). [...] At the southern extremity is a rich *Mihrâb*, or niche of marblework, to indicate the direction of Mecca for prayer. Close to this is a fine pulpit used on every Friday for preaching, and near that an elevated platform for the Pashà when he attends. Nearer to is, but lower, is the place for the Kâdi (Judge). On the other side of the church is the reserved place for women.

Nearly adjoining the *Mihrâb* on its east side is a chamber, with a marble niche beside it declared to have been the praying place of the Caliph Omar, and the true Mosque of Omar.

This (Church) Mosque of 'Aksa is very fine, but is has not the overwhelming interest of the other.

The pillars are inscribed with the names of Mohammed, Ali, Omar, Othmân, Abu Bekr, in letters of prodigious size. The capitals of many of the pillars are interesting, some being in basketwork and other peculiar patterns. [...]

Our hurried inspection was near its end. The Pashà was leading the way back, and we all followed, and found ourselves again in the open air upon the noble pavement, or esplanade; the lower, or outer, court of the Temple, with its small marble shrines, and a fountain (between the 'Aksa Mosque and the great Platform), with water from Solomon's Pools, among the trees. We were lost in astonishment at the beauty of the site – the Mount of Olives as seen from thence, and the Moab mountains – blue mountains just seen above the tips of the trees. [...]

The numerous visitors had, generally speaking, formed themselves into distinct groups: the Royal party was the nucleus of one company, the English bishop of another; each consul had his own circle of followers. No native Christians were there, all were Europeans.

Jews, even though in European costume, had no desire to enter the holy precincts so long as they remained defiled by the Gentiles, many of whose customs are in direct contrariety to the law of Moses: they believe that entrance thither will not be lawful till the locality be purified by the ashes of the red heifer (see Numbers XIX: 2) from the pollution of dead corpses in the ancient wars, and from the modern Moslem practice of bringing the dead there for prayers of the mourners previous to interment. [...]

We left the Sanctuary as we had entered it, escorted and guarded by the troops, the Pashà still leading the way through the small private door and passage of the Seraglio. [...]

We walked slowly home; the transactions of the day had been of supreme importance and delight, supplying food for mediation long after the immediate excitement was over. [...]

But when we thought of Jewish times and events, the place assumed its true importance in the mind. There was the central point of the Old Testament; there had been Solomon, Isaiah, Jeremiah, Ezekiel, the Lord Jesus Christ, Paul, Peter, and John, and on that Rock had been the Holy of Holies, before which the veil was rent as on yesterday (Good Friday).

The object of most importance to my feelings was that rock under the dome, the next, the scarped rock (at the NW point where we had emerged from the Seraglio and on which we had first set foot), and the section (perpendicular) of rock on the north side on which the barracks are built, and where Antonia must have stood; the next the view of the Mount of Olives and of the Moab mountains.

What an Easter eve this had been!

Bonfils, No. 280. Mosque of Omar: gate leading under the Rock. c. *1880.*
In the Jewish tradition, the Rock is where Abraham was going to sacrifice his son Isaac, until he was stopped by an angel. Centuries later King David brought the Ark of the Covenant to Jerusalem, but as a warrior he could not build a temple. He therefore appointed Solomon to build it; the temple was dedicated in 953 BC.

Photoglob, Zurich, PZ 1191. Mosque of Omar: entrance. c. 1895.
The Caliph Omar captured Jerusalem for the Muslims in 637.

*Mrs Dauglish Collection.
Jerusalem.* c. *1904.*
The area has a religious
significance for Jews, Muslims
and Christians. Compared to
the Church of the Holy
Sepulchre it was relatively free
of rivalries, which is perhaps
why Mrs Dauglish called this
view, simply, Jerusalem.

*Mrs Dauglish Collection. The
Mosque of Omar.* c. *1904.*
By the time this lantern slide was
made the instantaneous
photograph could add people to
the views, giving a greater sense
of reality.

Francis Bedford, No. 53. Mount Zion from the Governor's House. 1862.
The photographer added the following details to the caption to this unusual view: 'The group of buildings adjoining the tall
minaret is the residence of the Pasha.' The rooms on the right were for Muslim pilgrim scholars.

James McDonald. View of Mosque of Omar over gardens. 1864–5.

James McDonald. The Fountain of Saladin. 1864–5. The Egyptian Sultan Saladin conquered Jerusalem in 1187–9, followed by most of the Middle East. He restored the buildings on the Temple Mount and cleared the mounds of Crusader rubbish. In Roman times there had been a fountain on the Temple Mount, the water coming by a long and twisting aqueduct from the Pools of Solomon eight miles away. It was restored yet again in 1873 but only Muslims could use the water.

James Graham. Pulpit of ed-Din Kadr from the north-west. c. *1854.*
The Muslim pulpit, or *minbar*, when out of doors was of stone. It was aligned towards Mecca so that Muslims would be able to pray. Near El Aksa there was also a *minbar* ascribed to Saladin in the twelfth century.

James McDonald. Minaret at north-west angle and Barracks. 1864–5.
The Barracks, originally part of the Antonia Fortress, were the Jerusalem Governor's military headquarters at the northern end of the Temple Mount.

James Graham. Dome of Moses in the Holy Place from the south-east. c. *1854.*
The fig tree, allegedly planted by Muhammad, and the so-called Dome of Moses were west of the Dome of the Rock, near the Cotton Gate (Bab el Quattanum).

James McDonald. El Aksa Mosque from the south-east corner of the platform. 1864–5.
The El Aksa Mosque is the third most holy site to Muslims; only Mecca and Medina are more important. It is said
that one prayer in Mecca is worth 10,000 anywhere else; one at Medina equals 1000 and one at El Aksa 500.

Bonfils, No. 865. El Aksa Mosque. c. 1880.
The builder of the mosque is thought to be Al-Walid, son of
Al-Malik who is reputed to have built the Dome of the Rock.
Others suggest it was a Christian Church built in the time of
Justinian. It has suffered over the years. The Crusaders turned a
prayer niche into a urinal and in more recent times Mussolini added
inappropriate marble columns. Although extensively restored, it
probably looked its best at the time of this Bonfils photograph.

Zangaki, No. Z1213. Interior of El Aksa Mosque. c. *1885.*
The Crusaders captured Jerusalem in 1099 and slaughtered 40,000 Jews and Muslims. The mosque, as
Imad ad-Din reported, 'was a den of pigs and filth, crammed full of new buildings of theirs, occupied
by all manner of infidels, evil doers, oppressors and criminals.'

Bonfils, No. 865. Solomon's Stables,
south-east corner of Temple Mount. c. *1885.*
As in so many other cases in Jerusalem, it is not known if
Solomon actually stabled horses here. It is probable that
the arches were built in Herodian times to support an
extension of the Temple Mount. Behind the stables are
the huge vaulted water cisterns capable of storing millions
of gallons of winter rain underground.

James Graham. South-west corner of Temple platform with
Robinson's Arch and El Aksa Mosque. 1854.
Dr Edward Robinson, an American scholar/archaeologist, discovered the base of an
arch by the Temple Mount. Captain Warren later found a similar arch on the other side
of the valley suggesting that there was a bridge of about 40ft in span across the valley.

James Graham. Robinson's Arch. 1864.
The arch over the Tyropoeon Valley probably
was of great importance before the valley was
filled with about 30–60ft of rubble. The
masonry is similar to the Herodian stones of
the Wailing Wall, all of which were shaped
away from the Temple and later assembled.

The Jews

There are no accurate figures for the numbers of Jews in Jerusalem in the nineteenth century. Many were illegal immigrants and, like the Arabs, they wished to avoid the Turkish authorities. In 1845 the Prussian Consul gave the total population of Jerusalem as 16,410 of which 7,120 were Jews, 5,000 Muslim and 3,390 Christians (mostly Arab). These records show that there were also 800 Turkish soldiers and a mere 100 Europeans. In 1854 Karl Marx, then a journalist on the *New York Daily Tribune*, gave the total as 15,500 with 8,000 Jews and 4,000 Muslims. The latter he declared to be ' ... the masters in every respect'. Virtually all the land in the Old City was or had been owned by Arabs, even in the Jewish and Christian Quarters.

The 1868 *Jerusalem Almanack* shows for the first time the Jews becoming the dominant number. Out of a population of 18,000, Jews numbered 9,000, Muslims 5,000 and Christians, again mostly Arabs, 4,000. The same almanack numbers 21 synagogues, 11 mosques and 21 convents. In 1889 the total population, now spreading outside the Old City, was 39,175, with 25,000 Jews, 7,175 Christians and 7,000 Muslims.

The most interesting figures come from 1896 and give a total population of 45,472 with Christian Arabs 8,760, Muslim Arabs 8,600 and Jews 28,112. The Jewish population was divided between the following different groups – Ashkenazim 15,074; Sephardim 7,900; North Africans 2,420, Yemenites 1,288; Georgians 670; Bucharians 530 and Persians 230.

The conflict between the Ashkenazim and the Sephardim was intense. The British Consul James Finn wrote the following to his superiors in June 1849:

'The bitter dissensions among the various sections of Jews in this country is scarcely conceivable. The Sephardim (of Spanish descent and mostly Turkish subjects) regard themselves as the legal proprietors of the soil and actually compel the Ashkenazim (those from the East of Europe) to pay a territorial tax to them for the privilege of living in the Holy Cities. The former despise the latter and disdain to learn their vernacular dialect or to write their alphabetical character ... . Such instances [of conflict] show the deplorable state of Jews in Jerusalem, and this is mainly produced by their pauperized dependence on the nations of Europe for support, as the receipt and distribution of such funds is a fruitful source of discord. This habitual living on revenues from Europe has also induced the communities to contract enormous debts, which probably they would not have done had they been able to procure subsistence from handicraft employments.'

Sir Moses Montifiore was the most outstanding benefactor to Jerusalem. He retired at forty having made a fortune on the Stock Exchange. He became Sheriff of the City of London and was knighted by Queen Victoria. He was strictly Orthodox but found himself excommunicated for alleged errors. James Finn became a close friend and wrote to Lord Palmerston, the Foreign Secretary, in August 1849,

'Sir Moses has announced everywhere that his principal object was to ameliorate the condition of his people by the establishment of schools and trades, and by affording medical relief, among themselves and by themselves. But I regret to say that these benevolent designs have not met with the encouragement he had the right to expect …

'A more determined opposition however, was made to the establishment of schools for teaching European languages, geography, arithmetic etc. The rabbis denied the need of such things, especially of the Gentile languages, which would only expose then to the more seductive arguments of the Christian missionaries. They proclaimed that they, residing in the Holy Land and possessing the holy Talmud which comprises all science in its purest essence, had no need of such profane studies.'

Sir Moses was partially to prevail, and his windmill (originally built for grinding corn but now his museum) and his workers' cottages built outside the Old City now form artists' guest houses, Mishkenot Sha'ananm or 'The Dwellings of Tranquility'.

Another Jewish benefactor was much more sharp-tongued. The Austrian Dr Ludwig Frankl secured the support of the Elise von Herz Foundation to found a school for Jewish women. This was opposed to the extent that the Ashkenazim were prohibited from walking down the street past the school.

As well as the inter-sectarian conflict there were attacks on non-Jews. The brother of a converted Jew who had not himself converted was found in the Latin chapel of the Holy Sepulchre in April 1848. James Finn wrote: 'the multitude rushed upon him with the greatest fury … probably they would have murdered him but the [Turkish] Pasha came up, and, drawing his own sword, beat them back into the church.' Pashas varied in their attitude to Jews and to Christians. The greatest outrage was the slaughterhouse built in the Jewish Quarter, a source of pestilence and death. It was closed after the influential Sir Moses Montefiore put pressure on the Sultan in 1855.

There was also a high degree of benevolence towards the Jews from the British government. In January 1839 Lord Palmerston, the British Foreign Secretary, wrote to the Vice-Consul in Jerusalem that he should 'afford protection to the Jews generally'. A previous instruction of November 1838 had made it clear that this applied to foreign Jews, not native Jews. In practice it meant that Russian and Polish Jews (usually very orthodox) could, if renounced by their country of origin, become British Protected Citizens. They would thus be subject to British extra-territorial protection, rather than to the Turkish authority with its concomitant taxation and military service.

Huge numbers were not involved; in 1870 only 200 heads of families were recorded as protected, of which only 139 were in Jerusalem. However, the consulate records show that James Finn devoted a lot of his time to the protected subjects. Finn and his wife Elizabeth offered practical help to the Jewish community, establishing a plantation, managed by Elizabeth, for those who wanted to work. Mrs Finn also established Mrs Cooper's School for Jewesses, where 150 women worked in the morning and studied in the afternoon. At the peak of the Finns' activities, over 800 were involved in their institutions. The rabbis opposed these actions, including the treatment of Jews in the only hospital in Jerusalem because it was run by Protestants.

In July 1854 James Finn wrote: 'The Rabbis of Jerusalem have set themselves up to oppose, by every means in their power, any innovations upon the ancient routine of alms to be distributed by themselves … the high Rabbinical party will resist to the utmost the introduction of schools which will bring in modern feelings and render the people independent of their Talmudic authority.' This was not only the case with any Protestant proposals but was also found by Albert Cohn, an Austrian Jew and tutor to the children of Baron Rothschild, who wanted to establish a Jewish hospital and industrial schools. Even his proposal to distribute bread twice a week was opposed by the Rabbis.

The divisions between the Jews themselves were not simply between orthodox Ashkenazim and secular Sephardazim but within the groups themselves. The non-Jews looked at the terrible poverty of the Jewish pilgrims, who often became illegal settlers, and they also looked at the affluent life style of the Rabbis. Lady Frances Egerton in 1840 said of the wealthy Jews: 'Their homes are luxurious, clean and comfortable.'

Bonfils, No. 1220. The Wailing Place. c. *1885*
Because there were buildings close by, all views along the wall's
length had to be taken at an oblique angle.

Frank Mason Good, No. 579, published by Francis Frith, 1876. The Wailing Wall. 1866–7.
The wall's sacred status stems from the fact that the lower and larger stones were originally the Western Wall of Herod's Temple.

American Colony Photographer, No. 336. Ashkenazim Synagogue. c. 1900.
There was a time when Jews would not countenance photography because of the Commandment 'You
shall not make for yourself a graven image' (Exodus 20:4), but later this was related to the rest of the
Commandment dealing with the worship of idolatrous images.

James Graham. The Wailing Wall. 1854.
The most sacred place in Jerusalem for the
Jewish people. Before the State of Israel was
founded, numbers worshipping here were
comparatively small except during pilgrimages.

Carl Raad. (Gidal Collection.) A Persian Rabbi and his mother. c. *1900.*
The Persian explorer Cyrus captured Jerusalem in 537 BC and allowed Jews to return
from exile. However, over the centuries Persian Jews had enjoyed mixed fortunes so that
by 1896 there were only 200 Persian Jews in a Jewish population of 28,112.

Moses Ephraim Lilien. (Gidal Collection.)
Yemenite Rabbis study the Talmud. 1906.
The Pentateuch, as the Greek name suggests, were the five books of
Moses, the written basis of Judaism. The oral basis is the Talmud which
also derived from Moses and which was codified in about 500.

Moses Ephraim Lilien. (Gidal Collection.) Bukharian Jewish Girls. 1906.
In 1892 the Bukharian Quarter was home to wealthy Jews from Bukhara, an Asian province that became part of the Soviet
Union. The festive dress of the girls featured kaftans and colourful headdresses. Although their settlement outside the Old
City was called the Splendid Quarter, in the 1896 assessment they numbered only 530 of the 28,112 Jews in Jerusalem.

Anon. (Gidal Collection.) Heder or Jewish Grammar School. c. 1900.
Schooling for Orthodox Jewish boys began when they were four. They
learned the alphabet and, more importantly, daily prayers.

American Colony, Lewis Larson. An Ashkenazim Jew. c. 1905.
Orthodox Jews, particularly from Poland and Russia, came in increasing numbers in the nineteenth century; eventually they outnumbered the original Sephardic Jews from the Middle East. In 1896 the figures were 15,074 Askenazim and 7,900 Sephardim.

Photoglob, Zurich, PZ 15129.
Three Jews. c. 1885.
Many photographers paid little attention to authenticity, often choosing to call their subjects simply 'Jews' rather than be more specific.

Photoglob, Zurich, PZ 150245. The Wailing Wall. c. *1895.*
Even to this day only a certain style of local limestone can be used in
Jerusalem. In the evening sun it has a great warmth of colour. At this
time men and women prayed side by side.

George Washington Wilson Company.
A Jerusalem Jew. c. *1902.*
Wilson or one of his assistants probably took the original
photograph in the 1890s, while his company would have
made the coloured lantern slide soon after. At its peak the
company had 45,000 negatives from all around the world.

Arab Life

Many of the early trade routes from Europe to the Far East passed through the Ottoman Empire from Constantinople or Bursa to Aleppo and then from Baghdad down the Euphrates or Tigris to the Gulf of Oman and to India. There were other routes, including the Silk Route, where caravan journeys were measured in months or even years. The development of the overland route from Alexandria to Suez via Cairo became the favoured route to India. After the opening of the Suez Canal in 1869 the other routes faded into obscurity.

On one side of the Canal the Egyptian ruler was in financial trouble and was forced to accept British control. On the other side was the Ottoman Empire, 'the Sick Man of Europe', where European rulers gathered for the kill. The Russians gambled and lost on the Crimean War. The battleground was to be the Holy Land with Jerusalem its undisputed capital. The German Emperor made a triumphal entry into the city in 1898 with his geo-political aims barely disguised by the dedication of a Lutheran church.

The inevitable winner of the contest was Britain. In 1839 the influential British Foreign Secretary Lord Palmerston wrote to Vice Consul Young in Jerusalem saying that 'it will be part of your duty to afford protection to the Jews generally'. Young, replying, said 'There are two parties here who will doubtless have some voice in the future disposition of affairs, the one is the Jew − unto whom God originally gave this land for a possession − and the other, the Protestant Christian, his legitimate offspring. Of both Great Britain seems the natural guardian.' It is to be noted that there is no mention of the Arabs.

There are no reliable figures for the population of the Holy Land until after 1918, but the Prussian Consul in 1845 gave the figures as Muslims 5,000; Christians 3,390 and Jews 7,120. Since the Christians and the Muslims were both Arabs, they outnumbered the Jews. K. J. Asali quotes two figures. In 1849, Ottoman sources give the the following figures − Muslims 6,148; Christians 3,744 and Jews only 1,790. He also quotes Ben-Arieh with a third set of figures for 1850 − Muslims 5,350; Christians 3,650 and Jews 6,000. As any of these figures clearly show that the majority of the population were Arabs, why then were they ignored? One of the reasons was that the British government was only really interested in Protestants. A population figure for 1889 quoted by Martin Gilbert states that there were 300 Protestants, 4,000 Greek Orthodox and 2,000 Latins (Roman Catholics). The Greek Orthodox were mostly Arabs but all senior positions were filled by Europeans and much the same applied to the Latins.

Edward Said has collected some of the remarks made by Protestants about the Arabs. The Bishop of Salisbury told the PEF: 'Nothing I think that has been discovered make us feel regret at the suppression of Canaanite [i.e. Arab] civilisation … [The excavations show how] the Bible has not misrepresented at all the abominations of the Canaanite culture.' In 1874 the surveyor Tyrwhitt Drake wrote 'The fellahin are all the worst type of humanity that I have come across in the East …

The fellah is totally destitute of all moral sense.' The Dean of Westminster wrote of the 'singular union of craft, ignorance and stupidity, which can only be found in Orientals.'

It is in this context that the photographs of Hornstein have to be seen. Charles Alexander Hornstein was born a Christian in Jerusalem in 1870. His father Aaron was a Jewish convert and the owner of the Damascus Hotel, the second most important in Jerusalem. At the age of 15 he

Photoglob, Zurich, PZ 15115. Group of merchants from Siloam c. 1890 from 1870s sepia print.
The village of Siloam, now the Arab town of Silwan across the valley from the old city, was the local centre
of agriculture supplying most of the needs of Jerusalem.

had become Assistant Teacher at the Jerusalem Boys School where he had been educated. This was the missionary school for Jewish boys run by the London Society for the Promotion of Christianity amongst the Jews (London Jews Society). There he had come under the photographic influence of the headmaster G. Robinson Lees whose pictures were published and printed by the LJS in 1893 as *Bible Scenes in the Holy Land* and expanded in 1897 to *Village Life in Palestine*. From Lees, Hornstein

probably learned to photograph Arabs as they actually were. Earlier pictures by Bonfils and others had shown posed pictures of veiled anonymous women or groups frozen before the camera. With Hornstein we are not staring at subjects but rather are being given an insight into Arab life. For once the Arabs are not 'the worst type of humanity' but real people going about their legitimate business and, in one rare case (p. 121), even dignified by a name.

H. Tyler. Women grinding corn. c. 1890.
Tyler was a magic lantern slide maker and may have coloured and used
Francis Frith's originals from the 1850s.

Photoglob, Zurich, PZ 15113. Siloam milk women in the Jerusalem market. c. 1890.
Below Siloam village is the lower Pool of Siloam or Gihon, the site of a centuries-old cattle
market. Historically some of the animals on sale had been sacrificial, but by the 1890s it was
where milking cows were bought. The milk of goats and sheep was widely used, but
Europeans preferred the scarcer cows' milk.

Charles A. Hornstein. Ploughing. c. *1905.*
The Bedouin were the ever-moving shepherds, but the name *fellahin* was
given to the settled Arabs who cultivated the land.

Photoglob, Zurich, PZ 15118.
Arab merchant from Bethlehem on his
donkey. c. *1890 from 1870s sepia print.*
The market near the Jaffa Gate was held on
Fridays and many merchants would travel
the six miles from Bethlehem for this fair.

Charles A. Hornstein. Drawing water and water carrier. c. *1905.*
While winter rains filled the many cisterns under Jerusalem, the one
spring of fresh water provided work for many Arabs.

Charles A. Hornstein.
Reaping. c. *1905.*
The agricultural revolution was
still years away in the Holy Land.
Agriculture had changed little
from Biblical times.

Charles A. Hornstein.
Treading out corn. c. *1905.*
The harvesting method shown
here was similar to that used
throughout the Middle East.

Charles A. Hornstein.
Churning butter. c. *1905.*
The villages around Jerusalem,
particularly Siloam, supplied
milk for butter to be made in the
traditional way.

Charles A. Hornstein.
Destroying locusts. c. *1905.*
In everyday life the risk of a
plague of locusts was never
far away. The only solution
was to catch the insects and
destroy them.

Charles A. Hornstein. Women
carrying vegetables to market.
Below the Pool of Siloam was a
well-watered part of the Kidron
Valley where vegetables were
grown by local Arabs, to be sold
in the Jerusalem markets.

Charles A. Hornstein. Sheikh Khalil Senaah,
Christian tribesman from Kerak. c. *1905.*
In 1905 the Christian Arab population was 10,900, compared to 8,000
Muslim Arabs. The largest percentage belonged to the Greek Orthodox
Church. It was very rare for someone portrayed to be named.

Charles A. Hornstein. Woman carrying child. c. *1905.*
For Christian observers, the veiling or not of Arab women represented a
maze of contradictions, much depending on local traditions.

Charles A. Hornstein. Hunter and decoy. c. *1905.*
Relations between Arabs, Jews and Christians were better in Jerusalem
than anywhere else in the Holy Land, partly because the Arabs profited
from supplying food and water to the whole town.

Charles A. Hornstein. Two Arabs in traditional dress.
The school where Hornstein was headmaster took Arab pupils, and these could well have been the parents of pupils.

American Colony Photographer, No. 577.
Three veiled women. c. *1900.*
The formal dress and formal pose suggest the photograph
was taken in conditions demanding complete conformance
to tradition. Alternatively, they might be dressed for the
purpose of an exotic tourist souvenir.

Dr Conrad Schick, 146, No. 12. Muslim procession to the Tomb of Moses, Nebi Musa. c. 1870.
Moses is shared by Arabs, Jews and Christians but according to the Bible (Deuteronomy 34, 5–6) nobody knows his
burial place. In 1269 the Sultan Beybars created a 'tomb' on the Palestinian side of the Jordan as a place of pilgrimage and
a long procession came every year from Jerusalem for Easter, the Passover or both.

Anon. The Haldieh Library.
c. *1900.*
The Mamaluke rulers who
rebuilt much of Arab Jerusalem,
including the library, hoped
that the city would become a
major centre of Muslim
learning; the library was the
most notable success.

*American Colony
Photographer. Entrance to the
Haldieh Library.* c. *1900.*
An important Muslim library in
the Street of the Chain, dating
back to the fourteenth and
fifteenth centuries. The white
bands on the turbans are a sign
that the sheikhs have made the
pilgrimage to Mecca.

The Christian Churches

In the nineteenth century there was a strong compulsion to seek confirmation of the life and work of Jesus and even more importantly to verify the literal truth of the Bible. The focus of the indefatigable Mrs Dauglish's lantern slides shown to the many Temperance Societies and Sunday Schools were typical of the time. It is hard to conceive today the magic of the lantern slide show. At the time, there was no television, cinema or books illustrated by real photographs, and the darkened room with the bright colours of the lantern slide could hold the rapt attention of both young and old. There had been portfolios of monochrome prints before, but these were artistic albums for gentlemen connoisseurs. They certainly never reached children of the working class, the very class thought to be in most need of religious instruction.

At the time of the passing of the Education Act of 1870 only half the children in the country received any sort of elementary education and those who did were mostly in church schools. The Forster Education Act meant that, after 1870, the remainder of the children could receive an education in schools paid for by the local rates. These schools were non-sectarian but did provide 'simple Bible teaching'.

This 'simple Bible teaching' in the classroom was to be dominated by the lantern slide, but the stereograph also made an important contribution for smaller groups and for individuals without access to a magic lantern. The American firm Underwood and Underwood dominated the field. In 1900 they offered 'Palestine Tour No 1' and 'Palestine Tour No 2' (a total of 200 views), and from these they also extracted the 'Jerusalem Tour', 'Travel Lessons on the Life of Jesus' and 'Travel Lessons on the Old Testament'.

The stereos were packaged in book-like boxes with detailed notes and maps. The 'Jerusalem Tour' has 60 pages while 'Palestine Tour No 1' has 220 pages. In their self-advertising pages they stress their use in public schools and that they have been officially adopted by New York City, Boston and St Louis amongst others. They also quote from unsolicited letters of praise from the Pastor of St Andrews Church in New York and the General Secretary of the India Sunday School Union, who says 'This effective method of Bible study could be most profitably adopted in every church, institute, library, day school, Sunday school and home.'

There were also dozens of books with titles like *Pictures from the Holy Land* and *Lands and Peoples of the Bible*, even one bluntly entitled *Evidence of the Truth of the Christian Religion*. Significantly, H. V. Morton's bestseller was called *In the Steps of the Master*. The need for some sort of confirmation of religious belief was great in the nineteenth century. Darwin's *The Origin of the Species* (1859) had challenged the story of the Creation in Genesis and this had to be reconciled. In any large bookshop today, the many guides to Israel will be found in the travel section; yet in the religious section there are many more guides for pilgrims. *Come, See the Place* by Canon Ronald Brownrigg gives not only prayers for the appropriate places but even timings for pilgrimage walks.

The centre for Christian pilgrimage to Jerusalem was inevitably the Church of the Holy Sepulchre and the Via Dolorosa, of interest even to the most passive of Christians or casual tourist. There was a flurry of church building in the nineteenth century for a number of reasons. The church was obviously a place for ordinary worship but it also served as a centre for missionary work. In addition a church was a symbol of geo-political strength and could be used as a pawn in inter-church rivalries.

The first two British Protestant churches were missionary – Christ Church, built by the London Society for the Promotion of Christianity amongst the Jews, and St Paul's, built by the Church Missionary Society. The Anglican Cathedral of St George, built very much in the Victorian style, was completed in 1898.

Church building was not confined to the British. The Czar used the Russian Orthodox Church to support his claim for primacy over all Orthodox Christians, particularly the Greek Orthodox, though after his defeat in the Crimean

Bonfils, No. 256. Church of St Anne with two White Fathers. c. 1885.
The Romanesque church was built on the site of a Byzantine church by the Crusaders. It commemorates the place where
St Anne gave birth to the Virgin Mary. In 1856 the Sultan gave the church to Napoleon III of France. The earliest church had
been built on the site of the Pools of Bethesda. When captured by Saladin in 1192, it became a Muslim college.

War he focused his attentions more on religious than political aspirations, and built the spectacular Church of Mary Magdalene and the huge Russian Compound.

The most famous German church is Lutheran – the Church of the Redeemer, consecrated by the Kaiser himself and built, significantly, on the edges of the chapels of the Holy Sepulchre. On Mount Zion was the more recent German Benedictine Church of the Dormition. Other smaller religious dwellings were built. Near the Jaffa Gate was Deaconess House, a German Protestant mission and pilgrims' hostel opened in 1851. There was also a German Protestant orphanage founded in 1860, but biggest of all was the Templars or German Colony founded in 1871 outside the Old City.

Of particular photographic interest was the American Quarter or Colony. It was founded in 1881 by the Spaffords of Chicago, who devoted their lives to helping the poor. In addition they and their Swedish supporters founded a photographic department, and over 20,000 negatives are now held in the Library of Congress, providing probably the most reliable guide to photographic output that we have.

Zangaki, No. Z1201. Interior of the Church of St Anne. c. 1885.
As well as being regarded as one of the most beautiful churches, the Church of St Anne also has an impressive acoustic.
After the church was given to Napoleon III, he later gave it to the Brothers of the Algerian Mission, 'The White Fathers'.

James McDonald. North wall at the Pool of Bethesda. 1864–5.
In the courtyard of the Church of St Anne is the ancient pool where Jesus cured a
paralyzed man (John 5: 1–18) and was criticized for curing anyone on the Sabbath. The
first church built here was called 'the Church of the Lame Man', but this was destroyed
by the Persians in 614, to be followed by the Crusader church.

Zangaki, No. Z1297. Church of the Pater Noster. c. *1885.*
The present church on the slopes of the Mount of Olives was built in 1869 by a cousin
of Napoleon III, the Princess of Auvergne. Next to the church is a convent of Carmelite
nuns. Zangaki calls it the Chapel of the Ascension but it has been named for God the
Father since Byzantine times. The Lord's Prayer appears in the church 63 times,
in many different languages.

*American Colony Photographer, No 339. Anglican Church of
St George, near the Tomb of the Kings.* c. *1900.*
The Collegiate Church of St George was consecrated in 1898. Bishop
Blyth said at the time that it had become the central church for
Protestant worship. Unlike the earlier Anglican churches it is not
connected with any missionary society.

Carl Raad. (Gidal Collection.) The Armenian Patriarch. 1897.
Carl or Chalil Raad had been a pupil of the Armenian Garabed Krikorian, who in turn had been
a pupil of Yessayi Garabedian who took up photography around 1859. Yessayi became Patriarch
in Jerusalem in 1865 and, with a number of photographers, set up a commercial photographic
studio that flourished in the portrait trade.

Bonfils, No. 68. Russian Church on the Mount of Olives. c. *1890.*
The Russian Orthodox Church of St Mary Magdalene was built
by Czar Alexander III between 1885 and 1888. The golden domes recall
the Moscow of two centuries earlier and perhaps intentionally
dominate the view of the Mount of Olives.

Carl Raad. Greek Orthodox Priests in front of the Holy Sepulchre. 1913.
Because the chapels in the Church of the Holy Sepulchre had been allocated centuries previously, neither the
Protestants nor the Russian Orthodox Church are represented. The Greek Orthodox was indeed the major church
and this was of great concern to the Czars with their geo-political ambitions. However, the Greeks with their huge
Christian Arab population could resist all other claims.

Anon. (Gidal Collection.) The Russian Consul goes riding. c. *1910.*
There was not a great deal of social life in Jerusalem but one of the
forms of recreation was taking a ride into the countryside. This was
often a consular official's only contact with local people. He is seen here
guarded by his Kawass (centre). The Kawass was a sort of Major-domo,
linking the Europeans with the local population.

Anon. The Russian Hospice. n.d.
Tens of thousands of pilgrims of all religions flocked to
Jerusalem at Easter, Passover or the Nebi Musa – nearly all
were poor and many were sick. Czar Alexander II purchased
land outside the Old City in 1860. The 32 acres provided
basic accommodation for over 1000 pilgrims with a chapel,
reading rooms, refectories and hospitals. Besant and
Palmer, writing in 1871, were generous enough to describe it
in the following terms ' … for cleanliness and good
management it would compare favourably with any
institution of the kind in Europe.'

The Way Ahead

In 1850 Jerusalem had been a walled city crowded by 15–16,000 residents and pilgrims. By 1900 the settlements outside the walls stretched for a mile and a half and the population had risen to 50,000. By 1914 these settlements went on for two and a half miles and the now predominantly Jewish population numbered some 70,000.

Jerusalem had changed, and the change was made official by the Balfour Declaration of November 1917. Christopher Sykes has pointed out the attitude with which Balfour set about his task by quoting the words he wrote to the British Cabinet in August 1919: 'In Palestine we do not propose even to go through the form of consulting the wishes of the present inhabitants of the country.' The consequences of that decision are, mercifully, outside the scope of this book.

Another momentous event at this time was the discovery, in 1908, of oil near Solomon's Temple on the Persian Gulf. It was found by the company headed by William Knox D'Arcy, and was the first great oil strike in the area; this was doubly significant because the newly oil-fired warships of the Royal Navy were his customers.

1865 saw the opening of the telegraph office in Jerusalem, connecting the city to Jaffa and thus to the rest of the world. The successors of Consul Finn would be able to report back to Damascus, Constantinople or London. The dated dispatches of the British Consul give some idea of the time needed. A dispatch from Jerusalem dated 25 June 1849 was not acknowledged until 7 August; again, 7 August was the date of dispatch from the Foreign Office in London, not the date of receipt in Jerusalem. With such a time-scale needed, the Consul usually had to act on his own initiative. Probably this was a benefit because the Foreign Office rarely understood the intricacies of a local dispute; thus the arrival of more direct communication by telegraph was a mixed blessing.

Other forms of communication were also improving. The carriage road connecting Jerusalem to Jaffa was completed in 1886, but the work was badly done and soon had to be renewed. The metalled road to Bethlehem followed a few years later, going past the site of the future railway station. The rest of the roads remained as camel tracks. Since most of the transport on these tracks was by camel or donkey, this hardly mattered. However, the road to Jaffa was crucial to the future of Jerusalem because along it carts could bring building stones to feed the ever-increasing demand for construction materials in the settlements. It also made travel much faster and more secure. In the past a slow-moving cart had been an easy target for Bedouin robbers, but faster travel meant greater safety.

The light railway took four years to build and was eventually completed in 1892, but many travellers reported it underused until it was rebuilt by the British Army in 1918. (They built an aircraft runway at the same time, though commercial air travel was a long way off.) During the railway boom Jerusalem was connected via the Jaffa line to junctions with Gaza, Beersheba, Nablus and Haifa, and by the junction at Deras with Medina, Damascus and eventually Constantinople via Aleppo. It was a narrow-gauge, single-track line that snaked its way up from Jaffa. On the gradients it was so slow that in 1912 the Reverend J. E. Wright considered getting off the moving train, taking a photograph and then reboarding. The great value of the train was the transport of pilgrims.

Some of the most notable changes were in the Old City. The Sultan's Edict of Tolerance, issued in 1856 after the Crimean War, made a substantial difference to religious intolerance – it controlled the Pasha of Jerusalem so that, in theory, all religions became equal. The *status quo ante* decree in 1852 had already caused a reduction in religious rivalry. It was largely concerned with the ownership or administration of the Holy Places. Since the Church of the Holy Sepulchre, for example, was administered by six sects subdivided into more sects, there were constant disputes over demarcation lines. The decaying roof of the Holy Sepulchre was not repaired because of a demarcation dispute, and work was commenced only when the Sultan announced that he would pay for the repairs. (A more bizarre example is the ladder which leads to a window over the main entrance

and which has rested there for 150 years – no one will agree who should move it.) The indirect result was the great improvement in living conditions. Cesspools and slaughterers' charnel houses were closed down or greatly improved. The sewage problem was similarly improved and, most dramatically, so was the water supply. Since the earliest settlement Jerusalem had had a water problem. There was only one natural spring (at Siloam) and that was outside the city walls. The great majority of the population relied on rainwater collected in domestic tanks during the winter months and used throughout the rest of the year. Nearly every house seems to have had its own underground storage cistern, and there were huge public ones – the Sultan's Pool, the Upper and Lower Pools of Gihon, the Mamilla Pool, the Pool of the Patriarch. Another, Birket Israel, was lost until rediscovered by the PEF in 1869. It was over 100 yards long and held over three and a half million cubic feet of water. It was buried under rubble in spite of the fact that the pool was 80 feet deep. In the past it was thought by some to be the Pool of Bethseda, but this was nearby and also filled with rubbish.

The strangest history is perhaps Solomon's Pools eight or nine miles away beyond Bethlehem. There were three of them holding a total of 12.5 million cubic feet of water. Herod is said to have built the aqueduct to the centre of Jerusalem. It finished at the Temple Mount and, bizarrely, circled the Sultan's Pool. The later British pipeline could supply 280,000 gallons per day, perhaps comparable to the earlier aqueduct when that was working – unfortunately it was not often working.

The Romans were the first to restore it, while Lady Burdett-Coutts, 'the richest heiress in all England', was one of the most recent. The Baroness was noted for her many philanthropic works, but her offer to pay for the restoration of the aqueduct through the PEF came to nothing because of the indifference of the Turkish authorities. The aqueduct finished at a fountain in the Temple Mount, open only to Arabs who, according to Gidal, charged 3–5d per donkey-load of water. There were also huge reservoirs underneath the Temple Mount.

The poor condition of the water supply was the responsibility of the Turkish Pasha, who was in theory the public works contractor. The water supply in the Old City had been bad enough, but now that the city's population was expanding rapidly an improved supply was essential to that growth.

At the same time, the pilgrimage industry was in the process of transforming itself into a tourist industry. One of the principal causes was the company Thomas Cook and Son, with the son John Mason Cook being the prime mover. His first trip to the Holy Land was in 1868, when he took sixty

American Colony Photographer. (Gidal Collection.) Lepers begging for alms. c. 1900.
Leprosy was an incurable disease and lepers were forced to live in their own colony (Leviticus 13). The original colony in Jerusalem was in the Jewish Quarter but in 1887 the 'Jesus Leper Hospital', was built.

people. Finding that Jerusalem lacked good, large hotels, he decided to set up his own travelling camp. There were 21 sleeping tents with beds, carpets and tapestries and three dining tents with field kitchens, They were transported by 65 saddle-horses, 87 pack-horses and dozens of mules. The price for a 100-day tour of Egypt and the Holy Land was 150 guineas. Even the Kaiser's visit, which was supposed to demonstrate German superiority, was left in the hands of the Cooks. When the triumphant procession entered Jerusalem it was led by young Frank Cook. The party, which consisted of 105 in the royal party itself plus 108 Pashas and their servants with 1,430 horses and mules, camped just outside the gates. However, the age of the deluxe hotel and the package tour was just around the corner.

Picture postcards were introduced in Britain in 1899 and some of the old names reappear as publishers. Francis Frith was one, although he died in 1898. The 40,000 negatives he left to his company were mostly the work of his assistants. The other major publisher from the days of big prints was Valentines. James Valentine had died in 1880, well before the advent of this new format;

American Colony Photographer. Beggars. c. 1900.
Jerusalem was the city of poverty. A poor harvest could bring many of the Arab population to a level of poverty, while tax demands could force them to leave their homes and become beggars. Many of the Jews lived in greater poverty since thousands of older Jews had used their life savings to come to die in Jerusalem to be ready for the arrival of their Messiah. They lived on alms collected from their native countries and administered by rabbis. In 1851 W. H. Bartlett estimated that the amount they received was equivalent to £1.50 annually. A conversion to modern money is difficult, but this was poverty at starvation levels.

his firm was among the first to issue picture post-cards of Jerusalem.

The era of the photographic portfolio was over; as well as the postcard, at the beginning of the twentieth century the tourist was becoming increasingly a 'snapshotter' with his own Box Brownie and not in need of other people's photographs. In 1850 the British visitor to the Holy Land was usually well off, extending his Grand Tour to include Egypt and the Holy Land. The Polish or German visitor was usually the exact opposite – piteously poor and totally dependent on charity. In 1900 there were new classes of visitor, with the aristocratic British Protestant now more likely to be part of the ever expanding diplomatic corps and the tourist more from the budget-conscious middle classes.

It is clear that Jerusalem was moving into modern times. The new generation of photographers were more interested in the Zionist settlements than in the Biblical sites. Some, like Dawid Sabounji, photographed the Mikve Israel agricultural school. To these must be added, by strange irony, Charles Hornstein of the London Society for the Promotion of Christianity amongst the Jews.

American Colony Photographer, No. 518. Aged European Jews. c. 1900.
Ashkenazim Jews from Poland and Russia suffered most from poverty. In accordance with the Galuth, the banishment, the rabbis
restricted their life to prayer and the study of the Talmud. If they undertook work the rabbis said it would profane the Messianic life.

Edelstein. Jewish colony stables. c. 1908.
The caption adds that the scene is of Zillchron Yacob Samcreen, which is well north of
Jerusalem. It is an example of a model establishment, probably funded originally by
Baron Edmond de Rothschild.

Bonfils, No. 632. Wool corders in a Jewish colony. c. *1895.*
In spite of the rabbinical opposition, more and more Jewish settlers
took up work. The British Consul James Finn set up agricultural
settlements at Abraham's Vineyard in 1852 and at Taiybah in 1853.
By 1899 the census figures showed 2,576 families were supported by
workers and 615 families supported by alms. As always, the figures
are difficult to reconcile with a Jewish population in 1896 of 28,112,
but hopefully the proportions are reasonably accurate.

Frank Mason Good, No. 4310.
Interior of workshop, 1875.
One of the most famous pictures in the years
after the Crimean War was *The Shadow of*
Death by Holman Hunt picturing the young
Christ in the carpenter's shop. This
photograph by Good has a resonance with
the background of the painting.

Edelstein. Delivery of grapes. c. *1908.*
This is probably related to the earlier picture on p. 141, for Zillchron Yacob was an
extensive vineyard financed by Baron Rothschild. The hundreds of acres of vines
produced kosher wines exported mainly to America.

American Colony Photographer, No. 294. Native Tannery. c. *1900.*
'Native' in the context of the caption for this photograph is assumed to mean 'Arab'. The reliable
Bartlett places a tannery in 1843 on the Muristan near the Church of the Holy Sepulchre, which
together with the local cesspools made it ' … the most filthy and disgusting place in the whole of
the city – sufficient to breed a pestilence.'

Zangaki, No. 1257. The road to Bethlehem. c. *1890.*
The road from Jaffa was the first to be improved as a metalled road in 1868. The road to Bethlehem left from the Jaffa Gate. It was never built as such, but rather evolved over a period of time. Despite this its surface was smooth even before it was metalled.

Zangaki, No. 1143. Street view from the Hotel Hovarts. c. *1900.*
Right up until the end of the Great War, hotels were scarce in Jerusalem and had basic facilities. They changed their names as the various proprietors moved on. This is the view along the Jaffa Road and shows the studio of the Armenian photographer Garabed Krikorian.

American Colony, Lewis Larson. The road from Bethlehem. c. 1905.
This is the reverse view of the earlier photograph on p. 146 and is just about the first
sight a tourist would have of Jerusalem after arriving at the railway station.

*American Colony Photographer. View from the
south-west from road to railway station.* c. *1900.*
Another view of the station road. The growth of the
railway and proper roads was all-important in the growth
of Jerusalem, particularly outside the Old City.

*Garabed Krikorian, No. 3.
Railway cutting near Jaffa. 1891–2.*
The narrow-gauge railway was single-track with
passing places and a very convoluted path. Built
by French engineers, it was opened in 1892.

Garabed Krikorian, No. 5.
Railway bridge under
construction over
Wadi Sarar. 1891–2.
The Reverend J. E. Wright
called the train 'four trams
linked together and pulled by
an asthmatical steam-roller'.
It was so slow that on a steep
ascent E. A. Reynolds-Ball,
author of a 1901 guide book,
jumped out, picked flowers
and then rejoined the train!

American Colony
Photographer, No. 325.
Jerusalem railway station.
c. 1902.
The railway was just over 54 miles
long and the journey usually took
five hours. The fare in 1912 was
12s (60p) first class and 4s 2d
(21p) second class. The through
fare, including the train, from
London to Jerusalem return was
about £45 first class and £30
second class.

Zangaki, No. 1230.
The Pool of Hezekiah. c. *1885.*
Annie MacLeod described how
her father, on a pilgrimage in
1864, called on friends at the
Mediterranean Hotel which
overlooked the Pool of
Hezekiah: 'There the old
reservoir lay, immediately
beneath us, with its other sides
formed by walls of houses, their
small windows looking into it,
just as the one I gazed through
did.' Inside the traveller's room
were placards for Bass beers!

American Colony,
Eric Matson. Jerusalem in
the snow. c. *1910.*
If snow fell in Jerusalem it
was usually in December and
January, but snow has fallen
as late as Easter.

Dr Conrad Schick, No. 180. The opening of the aqueduct from Solomon's Pools. 1873.
The capacity of the three Solomon's Pools was 12,579,950 cubic feet. The aqueduct may have been built
by Herod but was restored by the Romans. It then fell into decay until Lady Burdett-Coutts gave
£50,000 to have it repaired. The aqueduct reopened in 1873 but closed soon after because of poor
workmanship. A Turkish pipeline was opened in 1901 but soon failed. It was the British troops in 1918
who finally established the first reliable supply.

Photographers' Biographies

American Colony (Swedish/American)

Horatio Spafford arrived from Chicago in 1881 and founded the Utopian community called the American Colony, soon to be joined by Swedish and Swedish–American pilgrims. The American Colony Hotel was established in 1902 in the luxurious palace of a Turkish Pasha and still exists today.

In 1898 two members from Nås in Sweden Lewis Larson and Erik Lind, with Elijah Meyers and Frederick Vester, started the photographic department. The Jerusalem-born German Vester, according to his daughter, was the seller of photographs at his gift shop near the Jaffa Gate, next door to Bonfils. At a later stage, some prints were issued by 'Vester and Co.'. Meyers was a converted Jewish Indian whose name never appeared on any prints, though it may be that Meyers took most of the early pictures. Also working with them, though he was not a member of the Colony, was Yashayuhu Raffalovich, a Russian Jew who produced the forward-looking 'Palestine and its Jewish Colonies' which he tried unsuccessfully to get published. There was also an American working on the book, who was a member of the Colony – John Whiting, whose photographs were mentioned in a court case. Also mentioned is Furman Baldwin, who was described as 'head of the Colony' and a photographer. The final figure in the group was G. Eric Matson (1888–1977), who came from the same town as Larson. He took over the business and changed its name to Matson Photo Service in 1934. He continued taking photographs until 1946 when he moved to America. In 1966, he eventually donated 20,000 negatives to the Library of Congress.

The Armenian Photographers

By 1860 the Armenian Christians had emerged as a major photographic force: the Abdullah Brothers were probably the most important photographers in Constantinople, and the official photographers to the Muslim Sultan.

Another significant photographer was the Armenian priest Yessayi Garabedian (1825–85), who founded a photographic portrait studio and went on to become the Patriarch of the Armenian church. His assistants were Father Yezekiel Kevork and Deacon Garabed Krikorian (1847–1920), both of whom were later to set up independent studios. Krikorian was an orphan born in Constantinople, whose earliest-dated photograph was taken in 1866. In 1885 he decided to marry, become a Protestant and open a studio near the Jaffa Gate. One of his competitors was Chalil Raad who was his rival for a while and then later his partner together with Krikorian's son Hovhannes, who had studied photography in Germany.

Antonio (Antoine) Beato, c. 1840–1905 (Italian)

Although he was in the Holy Land with his elder brother Felice and James Robertson, he appears not to have taken any photographs, and the proposed company – Robertson, Beato and Co. – fizzled out.

Felix (Felice) Beato, 1825–1908 (Italian)

See Robertson.

Francis Bedford, 1816–94 (English)

Bedford was in turn an architect, a lithographer and a photographer specializing in church architecture. He was one of the first to start systematically photographing large views of the whole of England. In 1862 Queen Victoria commanded him to accompany her son Edward, Prince of Wales, on his tour of the Middle East, together with Prince Alfred. The tour began in Cairo on 3 March 1862 and was carefully documented. During the next four months Bedford made 210 negatives. The earlier ones were made on Dr Hill Norris's plates and the later ones on wet collodion. The typical exposure was thirty seconds. From these, 172 prints were exhibited at the German Gallery, New Bond Street, to considerable acclaim. These were sold on subscription in 21 parts of eight pictures at 2 guineas with a final part of twelve prints at 3 guineas, totalling 45 guineas for the complete portfolio – 48 views of Egypt, 76 of the Holy Land and Syria, 48 of Constantinople, the Mediterranean, Athens etc.

The Bedford family were prosperous, Francis numbered no less than five admirals among his uncles and cousins. There was a family house on Southampton Row in Bloomsbury, where Francis was born. He bought a large house on Camden Road in north London in the 1850s and worked from there until he retired in the 1880s. His son William took over but died before his father; the business was then taken over by the manager, George Harris. The main output of the studio was Bedford's famous series of views of the British Isles. Bedford produced a huge number of prints, and was the innovator of a recycling method of recovering the silver from the development process.

Bonfils (French)

La Maison Bonfils was established in Beirut, Lebanon in 1867. Head of the family was Félix Bonfils, 1831–85, who founded the firm with his wife, Marie-Lydie Cabanais Bonfils, 1837–1919. It is thought that Félix travelled to take views while Marie-Lydie took the studio portraits. When Félix died in 1885, their son Paul Félix Adrien Bonfils, 1861–1929, joined his mother in the business. In 1895 Adrien left to open a hotel at Broummana, near Beirut. After World War I he left Lebanon for France. His mother continued the business until 1916 when she was evacuated by the United States Navy from Beirut to Cairo. Her assistant Abraham Guiragossian, possibly an Armenian from Palestine, took over and ran the business until about 1932. He published a

'Catalogue Général des Vues Photographiques de l'Orient'. Confusingly, Baedeker's *Palestine and Syria* (1894) says that the prints were being sold by Nicodemus in the Lebanon. All the prints were just signed Bonfils so it is not possible to work out which member of the family took them. They are numbered but not dated, and the only guide to dates is the 1876 catalogue complied by Félix Bonfils alone. The catalogue has four different numbers for each view according to format but the highest is 426 so presumably all the lesser numbers were taken by Félix before 1876.

The Bonfils family (and assistants) were enormously prolific, producing 15,000 views and 9,000 stereocards of Egypt, Syria, Greece and Lebanon in four years. They had branches or depots in Cairo, Alexandria, Baalbeck and Jerusalem. There is a similarity in backgrounds that suggests the company produced some slightly naughty nudes anonymously. Some Bonfils sepia prints were used by Photoglob in Zurich for their popular colour series.

John Cramb, born *c.* 1820 (Scottish)

The Royal Photographic Society had been founded in 1853 as the Photographic Society of London, and Cramb may have been one of the earliest members. From 1856 to 1879 he had a studio in Glasgow with his brother James. He became a member of the Photographic Society of Scotland and was Secretary of the Glasgow and West of Scotland Photographic Union.

He was commissioned by the well-known Glasgow publishers William Collins to take views of the Holy Land and 'objects of biblical interest and of scriptural association'. He used dry albumenised plates in a large '10 x 8' camera and two stereo cameras. He told the story of his travels in a series of articles in the *British Journal of Photography* in 1861. Collins published two books: *Jerusalem in 1860* with twelve photographic illustrations; and *Palestine in 1860* with 22 illustrations. The text was by the Reverend

Robert Buchanan, Moderator of the Church of Scotland, who had visited the Holy Land in 1857 and written about it. Cramb did not like Buchanan's text at all, calling it 'wholesale scepticism of continual sneering'.

Mrs Dauglish

Very little is known about Mrs Dauglish apart from the fact that she gave illustrated talks widely among the Temperance Societies (and probably Sunday Schools) of the nineteenth century. Given an occasional date on a photograph and some clues within the photographs themselves, it is possible to work out that she was accumulating photographs at least from 1904 to 1931. In this long period it seems that Mrs Dauglish took many of the pictures, obviously the family snaps, but also that she bought in many others. Francis Frith, Frank Mason Good and George Washington Wilson have been identified, even though the original photographs were taken decades before Mrs Dauglish's lantern slides were used. Many of the slides have been coloured, at times more wishfully than accurately.

Edelstein

Nothing is known about him except that he may have been a Jewish convert to Christianity. Some photographs appear belatedly in *Walks Around Jerusalem* which was published in 1926 by the Reverend J. E. Hanauer.

Luigi Fiorillo (Italian)

Even in his lifetime there was confusion between L. Fiorillo and F. Fiorillo. They may have been brothers or indeed father and son. They were both based in Egypt. Luigi Fiorillo had a studio in Alexandria and published *Alexandria in Ruins* in about 1882–3 following the bombardment and rioting. Luigi exhibited in Naples in 1871 and in Paris in 1878. F. Fiorillo photographed the first Aswan Dam in 1905 and had a studio in Khartoum and possibly Aswan. Luigi made at least one visit to the Holy Land and was photographer to the Russian Imperial Orthodox Palestine Society. Some of the later photographs are signed 'V. L. Fiorillo et Fils' or, confusingly, others are signed 'Marquis and Fiorillo'.

Francis Frith, 1822–98 (English)

He was by far the most successful and prosperous of all the photographers of the Near East. His father, a Quaker, was a cooper in Chesterfield. After serving an apprenticeship, Frith worked for five years in a factory before he suffered a nervous breakdown. On doctor's orders, his parents took him on a two-year tour of Britain. In 1845 he moved to Liverpool where he ran, in partnership, a prosperous wholesale grocery business. Tiring of this after five years, he sold up and started an even more prosperous printing business. In 1853 he took up photography and in 1856 sold the printing firm. At 34 years of age he was a gentleman of leisure with ample means.

In September 1856 he made his first trip to Egypt, Nubia and the Holy Land, returning in July 1857. His equipment included one additional large and one stereo camera. His companion was Francis Wenham, optical adviser to Negretti and Zambra, who eventually published Frith's stereo photographs. Frith signed and dated many of the early prints; some have only the name Frith printed on the mount, and it is possible that they were taken by Frank Mason Good. On his second tour, from November 1857 to May 1858, he again visited the Holy Land, Syria and the Lebanon.

Obscurity surrounds his third and final trip to the Middle East and it is difficult to pinpoint the results as these photographs are not dated like the earlier ones. It is usually said that the trip was in the summer of 1859. This is unlikely, since any experienced traveller to Egypt and Nubia would have known that the heat would be intolerable.

Following his marriage in July 1860 he began his monumental work of photographing every town and village in Britain: the work still survives today.

Frank Mason Good, 1839–1928 (English)

Good was born in Deal, Kent and was trained by his father as a druggist and chemist. From 1866 to 1877 he lived in London and worked as a photographic chemicals manufacturer. It has been suggested that he was an assistant to Francis Frith, but he did travel independently and later sold his prints to the Frith publishing company. Bertrand Lazard has disentangled Good's four Middle East trips: 1866–7 Egypt and the Holy Land, published Frith 1876; 1868–9 Egypt and Nubia, published Mansell; 1871–2 Egypt, Constantinople and Malta, published Frith; 1875 Holy Land, published Mansell and by Good himself. Lantern slides were also published by the Woodbury Publishing Company and apparently by the George Washington Wilson company.

James Graham, 1806–69 (Scottish)

Graham became Lay Secretary for the London Society for the Promotion of Christianity amongst the Jews (usually called the London Jews Society) in 1853. He resigned his post in 1857 and travelled to Egypt and back to Jerusalem, before returning briefly to London and then finally settling in Paris. He used paper negatives but made no attempt to sell prints. A very rare album containing 82 prints and five panoramas, which he had presented to his sister Elizabeth, was auctioned at Christie's in 1989. His photographs appeared in several books – *The New Testament* (1865), *Scenes of the East* by the Reverend H. B. Tristram (1870), *The Holy Land* by W. H. Dixon (1865), *The Land of Sacred Mystery* by Reverend W. L. Gage (1871) and *Eastward* by N. MacLeod (1866).

As well as his room at the London Jews Society, he took a room at the very top of a tower which was in turn at the top of the Mount of Olives. This was very popular in summer when the air of Jerusalem could be quite suffocating, and the room was used by several painters including William Holman Hunt and Thomas Seddon.

In 1849 Elizabeth Finn, the wife of the British Consul, asked a friend in London to send her photographic apparatus for talbotypes i.e. using paper negatives. She intended to make prints to sell for her various charities but found that she did not have enough time for the enterprise. Graham apparently heard about her attempts and so brought a camera with him when he came out in 1853. Soon he was supplying prints to Mrs Finn who sent them back to London. Graham also bought her camera and gave it to Mendel Diness. Graham taught him how to use it and Diness became the first Jerusalem resident photographer.

It is not known why Graham resigned but when back in London he and Holman Hunt wrote a damning criticism of the Mission School and in particular of its head, Bishop Gobat. After a period in London and Paris he spent a lot of time in Italy. Holman Hunt adds to the little that is known about him by saying that Graham had been the director of a failed Glasgow bank; this financially ruined him and had led to his life in photography.

W. Hammerschmidt (German)

Hammerschmidt began work in Berlin and was awarded a medal in the Berlin Exposition of 1863. From 1862 onwards he exhibited as a member with the Société Française. He had a studio and shop in Cairo from 1861 and over the years exhibited a range of sound, well-made views of both antiquities and street scenes. Many of his images were used by Photoglob, Zurich and probably by postcard makers. He was shot and wounded while photographing pilgrims to Mecca. He returned to Berlin where he apparently continued to maintain a studio in his later life.

Charles Alexander Hornstein, b. 1870, d. after 1932 (Palestinian)

Hornstein was born in Jerusalem of Christian parents. His father Aaron was a Jewish convert and was probably, like his brother Moses, born in

Germany. In the 1870s they were both hotel owners. Aaron owned the Damascus and Moses the better-quality Mediterranean. Charles' mother was Jessie Gatherer, the Scottish nursery governess of Mr and Mrs Finn, the British Consul and his wife.

Hornstein was educated at the Jerusalem Boys School, otherwise called the LJS Mission School and formerly called Bishop Gobat's School. The headmaster then was G. Robinson Lees – a noted photographer. At the age of 15 Hornstein was appointed assistant teacher at the school. He eventually became headmaster, from which time his life seems to have been very quiet except during World War 1 when he had to teach under appalling conditions. He appears to have married in 1897 and had a son and a daughter.

G. Robinson Lees BA, FRGS, b. 1860 (English)

Lees was headmaster of the Jerusalem Boys School before Charles Hornstein and was also one of the most interesting photographers of the time. *Jerusalem Illustrated by Original Photographs* was illustrated with twelve of his photographs and was the first book ever published in English in Jerusalem. His other books include *Pictorial Palestine – Ancient and Modern* and *Bible Scenes in the Holy Land*. He also published *Village Life in Palestine* in 1905. As the title suggests, it consists of views of Arab life, seen sympathetically. In later editions, published when Lees returned to England, his old photographs were supplemented by more recent ones by Charles Hornstein.

Sergeant James McDonald RE, 1822–85 (Scottish)

McDonald, born in Edinburgh, enlisted in the Royal Sappers and Miners in 1839 and soon transferred to the Ordnance Survey. He purchased his discharge in 1845 when he worked as a civil engineer during the 'Railway Mania'. In 1846 he rejoined the Ordnance Survey as a civilian but re-enlisted in 1849. By 1855 he was promoted to

Sergeant and appointed photographer in the map room. The Royal Engineers were taught photography at the School of Military Engineering, Woolwich, after the Crimean War. William Abney (1843–1920) was a Lieutenant of the Royal Engineers and is believed to have been the teacher. Abney went on to become an important chemist in photography, and President of the Royal Photographic Society from 1892; he was a prolific writer on technical matters. In 1864 Captain (later Colonel Sir) Charles Wilson selected Sergeant McDonald as senior NCO for the survey of Jerusalem and Sinai. Promoted to Regimental Sergeant Major, he was summoned by Queen Victoria to Osborne on account of 'his many beautiful photographs'. He was commissioned Quartermaster in 1869 and retired in 1881 with the rank of Honorary Captain, to live in Dublin. His official trade was bookbinder and printer. He died in Southampton on 31 October 1885. His obituary pays tribute to the 45 years he worked for the Ordnance Survey but adds enigmatically that his connection continued 'until the day of his death'.

He is usually associated with Corporal (later Master Sergeant) Phillips (b. November 1831) who also worked with the Ordnance Survey in Palestine. Phillips, described officially as a carpenter, retired in 1874 to live at South Camp, Aldershot.

Photoglob, Zurich (PZ)

The PZ photographs are renowned for their famous brilliant colouring. The process called Photochromy was developed in Zurich by Orell, Füssli and Co. in 1887. The English Photochrom Company was not formed until 1896. It produced vast quantities of postcards but no large photographs, and neither were to the same standards as the Zurich company. The process is not colour photography, but rather the use of colotype photolithography with a solution of asphaltum of ether, and involves as many as sixteen printings of different colours. The PZ prints of the Holy Land were made from photographs or negatives of several photographers, including Zangaki or more usually Bonfils. Exactly the same typography and numbering was used by the company Edit. Schroeder & Cie., Zurich, who may have been connected but only published monochrome prints.

Chalil (or Carl) Raad, b. 1869 (Lebanese)

It is probable that Raad took the European name Carl for commercial reasons. He was a Christian and possibly, given his companions, an Armenian Christian. He settled in Jerusalem in 1890 and was assistant to, and pupil of, the deacon of the Armenian church, Garabed Krikorian. In 1897 Raad had his own studio near the Jaffa Gate. Raad's studio was directly opposite Krikorian's and his ex-teacher was now his rival. This continued until 1913 when Krikorian's son Hovhannes returned from studying photography in Germany and took over the studio. He also married Raad's niece and the businesses combined. Some 1,263 of Raad's negatives were presented by his daughter to the Institute for Palestine Studies and were used extensively to illustrate the book *Before the Diaspora – A Photographic History of the Palestinians, 1876–1948*. Part of his archive was reported destroyed in the 1948 war.

James Robertson, 1813–88 (Scottish) and Felice Beato, 1825–1908 (Italian)

James Robertson was a Scotsman, though he was born in London. He was trained as a coin engraver by William Wyon, Chief Engraver to the Royal Mint, London. In 1841 he arrived in Constantinople as Chief Engraver to the Turkish Imperial Mint. The salary was a handsome £40 a month. Around 1854 he started photographing in Greece and Constantinople, and more famously during the Crimean War. His photographs were received with acclaim in London. Sometime in

1854–5 he met the Beato family. He married Maria Matilde Beato on 19 April 1855 in Constantinople and their first child Catherine Grace was born in 1856. Two other daughters were to follow. At about this time he went into partnership with Maria's brother Felice (or Félix). The first probable assignment for Felice on his own was to the Scutari graveyard in August 1856. Robertson and Beato's next major expedition was to the Holy Land via Egypt. They arrived in Jerusalem on 3 March 1857 and were accompanied by Felice's younger brother Antonio who does not seem to have taken an active part, although the signing of some of the photographs as Robertson, Beato and Co. obviously anticipated that there would be a third party. This was never to be. Following this trip Robertson went back to Constantinople and never photographed again. Felice went to India, then China, Japan and Burma. Antonio went to India to run a depot for Felice but soon returned to Egypt because of his health.

The published catalogue from their Jerusalem trip contains 32 prints, all of the usual sights and all (bar three or four) within the square mile of the Old City. In October 1857 Robertson seems to have been advertising the sale of his business in *The Levant Herald,* but the sale seems to have failed as some or all the negatives were passed to Felice Beato.

Dr Conrad Schick, 1822–1901 (German)

It is not clear whether Dr Schick took the photographs himself as it seems more likely that he instructed a camera operator. His images, like the man, are quite remarkable. He was born in Germany and was one of four missionaries from a Swiss mission to come to Jerusalem in 1846. Schick became head of the School of Industry run by the London Jews Society to teach carpentry and other trades to young Jews. He seems to have run the school and its associated printing works for fifty years but he was also fascinated by the architecture of the city. In 1848 he investigated the newly discovered Solomon's Quarries and for many years was the very welcome helper to the archaeologists of the PEF. Perhaps his greatest moment came when one of his pupils – Jacob Eliyaha, later adopted into the American Colony – was playing near the Siloam Pool and discovered an ancient inscription on the wall of a tunnel. This turned out to be an account of the building of Hezekiah's Tunnel connecting the Gihon Spring and the Siloam Pool and was a very valuable contribution to the historical study of Jerusalem. He excavated in that area from 1886 to 1900 but will be remembered most for the help that he gave to others. He was also well known for his models of the buildings which had been destroyed centuries earlier.

Underwood and Underwood (American)

In 1882 20-year-old Elmer Underwood and his 18-year-old brother Bert expanded their book-selling agency to become agents for stereocards west of the Mississippi River. Their base was Ottowa, Kansas and by 1891 they had expanded to Baltimore and New York. In 1891 Bert took camera lessons from a Mr Abel in France and over the next few years photographed in Italy, Greece, the Holy Land and Egypt. By 1901 they were producing 25,000 stereocards a day and selling 300,000 viewers a year. Their salesmen concentrated on school superintendents, public librarians and the town bankers. Production was discontinued in 1920 and in 1921 the stock and rights were sold to the Keystone View Company.

The 27 Jerusalem stereos were sold in a box shaped like two books. The cards had the title and copyright under the picture on the front, the title was repeated in six languages on the back and was sometimes accompanied by some explanatory text. The box also contained a 100-page booklet for the images. The booklet included a map of Jerusalem which showed not only the important sites but also the camera positions and the angles of view of the various shots.

George Washington Wilson, 1823–93 (Scottish)

Wilson was apprenticed as a carpenter in his native Scotland but he showed a natural talent for painting, and after training in Edinburgh became a miniaturist.

In 1849 he settled in Aberdeen as an artist and teacher of painting but by 1853 had diversified into a partnership with John Hay Junior in photographic portraiture. The partners were also commissioned by Prince Albert to make photographs showing the stages of construction of the Royal Palace of Balmoral, for which Queen Victoria was eventually charged £25 4s. By 1880 his partnership had been dissolved and Wilson ran the company himself, but by this time his company was one of the largest, supplying tourist photographs not just of Scotland but the whole of Britain, with a stock of 45,000 negatives. The Wilson company expanded its business outside Britain, and there were catalogues for South Africa, Gibraltar, the south of Spain and Morocco. The Wilson company seems to have bought photographs in, and there is a possibility that some of the GWW lantern slides of Jerusalem may actually have been taken by Frank Mason Good.

Zangaki Bros. (Cretan or Cypriot)

Their photographs are always signed with no more than the word 'Zangaki'; this has a curious 'Z' that in the past has been mistaken for an 'L'. One bowler-hatted brother appears in some pictures beside their darkroom van, on which their name appears in English and Arabic, although their photographs are all captioned in French.

The Zangaki brothers are said to have had a studio in Port Said, but it seem that by the mid-1890s they may have sold out to Peredis. The brothers were noted not only for their views but also for depicting native life. Their photographs of the Holy Land are rare but the PEF inherited some original negatives.

Select Bibliography

Allen, William, "Sixty-nine Istanbul Photographers 1887–1914", in Kathleen Collins (ed.), *Shadow and Substance. Essays in Honour of Heinz Henisch* (Pennsylvania: Amorphous Institute Press, 1990).

Asali, K. J. (ed.), *Jerusalem in History* (London: Scorpion Publishing, 1989).

Atkins, Norman, *Jerusalem: An Insight City Guide* (Singapore: APA Publishing, 1989).

Bamm, Peter, *Early Sites of Christianity* (London: Faber and Faber, 1957).

Bedford, Francis, "Photographic pictures taken during the tour of the East (with HRH The Prince of Wales)", originally published in 1862, facsimile edition, *The RPS PhotoHistorian*, Supplement 122/3, 1998.

Blumberg, Arnold, *A View from Jerusalem 1849–58: The Consular Diary of James and Elizabeth Anne Finn* (London and Toronto: Fairleigh Dickinson University Press, 1980).

Brownrigg, Ronald, *Come See the Place: A Pilgrim's Guide* (London: Hodder & Stoughton, 1988).

Buckland, Gail and Vaczek, Louis, *Travellers in Ancient Lands* (Boston: New York Graphic Society, 1981).

Buonaventura, Wendy, *Serpent of the Nile: Women and Dance in the Arab World* (London: Saqi Books, 1989).

Chevedden, Paul, *The Photographic Heritage of the Middle East* (Malibu: Undena Publications, 1981).

Cramb, John, "Palestine in 1860", *British Journal of Photography*. Twelve articles from 16 Dec 1861.

Darrah, William C., *The World of Stereographs* (Gettysburgh: W. C. Darrah, 1977).

Elon, Amos, *Jerusalem: City of Mirrors*, revised edn (London: Harper Collins, 1996).

Erbstösser, Martin, *The Crusades* (Newton Abbot: David & Charles, 1978).

Finn, Elizabeth, *Reminiscences of Mrs Elizabeth Finn* (London and Edinburgh: Marshall, Morgan and Scott, 1929).

Finn, James, *Stirring Times: Jerusalem Consular Records* (London: Kegan Paul, 1878).

Gavin, Carney, *The Image of the East* (Chicago: University of Chicago Press, 1982).

Gilbert, Martin, *Jerusalem: Rebirth of a City* (London: Chatto and Windus, 1985).

—, *Jerusalem in the Twentieth Century* (London: Chatto and Windus, 1996).

—, *Jerusalem: Illustrated History Atlas*, revised edn (Jerusalem: Steimatzky, 1978).

Goldstron, Edward, "The British Consulate in Jerusalem in relation to the Jews" in Albert Hyamson (ed.), *Palestine* (The Jewish Historical Society of England, 1941).

Glotman, Joshua, 'Ideals in Early Palestinian Postcards', unpublished manuscript, 1980.

Graham-Brown, Sarah, *Images of Women: The Portrayal of Women in Photography of the Middle East 1860–1950* (London: Quartet Books, 1988).

Hallan, Elizabeth (ed.), *Chronicles of the Crusades* (Godalming: Bramley Books, 1997).

Harper, Henry A., *Walks in Palestine*, new edn (London: Religious Tract Society, 1894).

Henisch, B. A. and H. K., "James Robertson of Constantinople: a chronology", *History of Photography*, vol. 14, no. 1 (1990).

Hershkowitz, Robert, *The British Photographer Abroad. The First Thirty Years* (London: Hershkowitz, 1980).

Holman Hunt, W., *Pre-Raphaelitism and the Pre-Raphaelite Brotherhood* (London: Macmillan & Co., 1905).

Jammes, Isabelle, "Louis Désiré Blanquart-Evrard 1802–1872", *Camera* (Lucerne: C. J. Bucher, 1978).

Jay, Bill, *Victorian Cameraman* (Newton Abbot: David & Charles, 1973).

—, "Francis Bedford 1816–1894", *Bulletin of the University of New Mexico*, no. 7, 1973.

—, "Up the Nile with Francis Frith, Francis H. Wenham 1824–1908", *Northlight 7: Forgotten Victorians* (New Mexico, 1977).

Join-Lambert, Michel, *Jerusalem*, trans. from

French (London: Elek Books, 1958).

Kenyon, Kathleen M., *Digging Up Jerusalem* (London: Ernest Benn, 1974).

—, *Archaeology in the Holy Land*, 2nd edn (London: Ernest Benn, 1965).

Kollek, Teddy and Pearlman, Moshe, *Jerusalem* (Jerusalem: Steimatzky, 1968).

Lazard, Bertrand, "The Photographs of James Graham in the Middle East", *RPS PhotoHistorian*, Supplement 89, 1990.

Macleod, Annie C., *Half Hours in the Holy Land* (London: James Nisbet). Based on her father's "Eastward", a journey made in 1864.

Miraglia, Marina et al., *Frederico Peliti: An Italian Photographer in the Time of Queen Victoria* (Manchester: Cornerhouse, 1994).

Morton, H. V., *In the Steps of the Master* (London: Rich and Cowan, 1934).

Lang Neil, C., *Pictorial Palestine: Ancient and Modern*, contributions and photographs by Rev. G. Robinson Lees (London: Miles and Miles).

Nir, Yeshayahu, *The Bible and the Image: Photography in the Holy Land 1839–1899* (Pennsylvania: University of Pennsylvania Press, 1985).

Onne, Eyal, *Photographic Heritage of the Holy Land 1839–1914* (Manchester: Manchester Polytechnic, 1980).

Osman, Colin, "New light on the Beato brothers", *British Journal of Photography*, 134, 6636, 16 October, 1987.

—, "The Beato brothers, an attempt at nomenclature", *RPS Historical Group Quarterly*, 79, Winter 1987.

—, "Postcards from Egypt", *RPS Historical Group Newsletter*, 64, Spring 1984. (About the Zangaki brothers.)

—, "Black and white postcards", *Creative Camera*, 226, 1983.

—, "The later years of Felice Beato", *The RPS Photographic Journal*, November 1988.

—, "Felice Beato: A Chronology (with others)", in John Clark, *Japanese–British Exchanges in Art* (London: School of Oriental and African Studies, 1989).

—, "Fact and Fiction about the Life of Felice Beato", in Deiter Sigurt, *Felice Beato in Japan 1863–73* (Heidelburg: Editions Braus, 1991).

—, "The later years of James Robertson of Constantine", *History of Photography Journal*, Spring 1992.

Perez, Nissan, *Focus East: Early Photography in the Near East 1839–1885* (New York: Abrams, 1988).

Pudney, John, *Suez, de Lessep's Canal* (London: J. M. Dent, 1968).

Roberts, David, *From an Antique Land: Lithographs of Egypt and the Holy Land (1842–49)*, with comments from his unpublished journal (London: Weidenfeld and Nicolson, 1989).

Said, Edward, *Orientalism* (London: Routledge & Kegan Paul, 1978).

—, *Culture and Imperialism* (London: Chatto and Windus, 1993).

—, *The Question of Palestine*, revised edn (London: Vintage Books, 1992).

Schölch, Alexander, *Palestine in Transformation 1856–82* (Washington DC: Institute for Palestine Studies, 1993).

Searight, Sarah, *The British in the Middle East*, revised edn (London: East–West Publications, 1979).

Smith, William, *A Dictionary of the Bible*, revised edn (Michigan: Zondervan Publishing, 1970).

Taylor, Roger, *George Washington Wilson* (Aberdeen: Aberdeen University Press, 1981).

Valentine, L., *Palestine, Past and Present, Pictorial and Descriptive* (London: Frederick Warne).

Van Haaften, Julie, *Egypt and the Holy Land in Historic Photographs* (New York: Dover Publications, 1980).

—, "Francis Frith and Negretti and Zambra" *History of Photography Journal*, 4 Jan 1980.

Vilnay, Zev, *Legends of Jerusalem* (Philadelphia: Jewish Publication Society of America, 1977).

Wachlin, Steven et al., *Images of the Orient* (Rotterdam: Museum voor Volkenkunde, 1986).

Wahrman, Dror, Gaven Carnet and Rosovsky Nitza, *Capturing the Holy Land* (Harvard Semitic Museum, 1993).

Wardle, J., *A Tour to Palestine and Egypt and Back* (Nottingham: H.B. Saxton, 1907).

Wilkinson, Charles, *Holy Land Pilgrimage* (Toronto: Pilgrim Paperbacks, 1984).

Wilson, Derek, *Francis Frith's Travels* (London: Dent, 1985).

Wright, Reverend J. E., *Round About Jerusalem* (London: Jarrolds, n.d. *c.* 1918).

Further Reading

Most of the photographs in this book came from the archive of the Palestine Exploration Fund, which means that some well-known names do not appear for the simple reason that their pictures are not in the archive. On the other hand, some little-known photographers who have produced superb photographs are well represented.

I have also drawn on the work of Tim Gidal, who I was fortunate enough to meet in 1979 in Israel and to work with for a brief time. It seemed natural to me to ask his widow Pia for items from his collection to add to the PEF images, because I felt the book would benefit from the portraits and the human touches exhibited in his own collection. His own photographs are now beginning to be given the credit they deserve and I am only sorry that all of them fell outside the time-span of this book. However, I unreservedly recommend his books, a few of which are listed below.

Gidal, Nachum Tim, *Eternal Jerusalem – A Portfolio of Historic Photographs* (Tel Aviv: Steimatzky, 1980).

—, *Jerusalem in 3000 Years* (Cologne: Könemann, 1995). The text is in English, German and French. The book contains 400 photographs, the modern ones are mostly taken by Dr Gidal.

—, *Land of Promise: Palestine 1850–1948* (Tel Aviv: Steimatzky, 1985).

—, 'Exhibition Catalogue' (Tefen, Israel: The Open Museum, 1992). The text is in English and Hebrew and there is a detailed bibliography.

Ariel Books are a series of inexpensive books edited by Ely Schiller and published in Hebrew and English by Ariel Publishing, Jerusalem. They provide a treasure trove of rarely-seen images that with a little effort can be identified by author. These titles are:

Schiller, Ely (ed.), *The First Photographs of Jerusalem: The Old City* (Jerusalem: Ariel Publishing, 1978).

—, *The First Photographs of Jerusalem: The New City* (Jerusalem: Ariel Publishing, 1979).

—, *The First Photographs of the Holy Land* ((Jerusalem: Ariel Publishing, 1979).

—, *The First Photographs of Jerusalem and the Holy Land* (Jerusalem: Ariel Publishing, 1980).

Also published by Ariel Books is a 1976 reprint with a slight rearrangement by Zev Vilnay of Colonel Sir Charles Wilson's *Picturesque Palestine* first published in 1880. Although many of the engravings that illustrate it do not give the source of the image, it remains an important document. The four volumes are *Jerusalem – the Holy City*; *The Land of Judea*; *The Land of Galilee*; *Sinai (including Petra)*.

Ariel have also reprinted the original Ordnance Survey maps and photographs.

Index

Numbers in italics refer to photographs.